REGENCY LONDON

Overleaf. Above: Horwood's *Plan of the Cities of London and
Westminster*, published 1794, showing the Parish of St Marylebone.
Below: two views of the country north of the New Road from Paddington
to Islington, also dating from 1794.

REGENCY LONDON

Stella Margetson

PRAEGER PUBLISHERS
New York · Washington

BOOKS THAT MATTER

Published in the United States of America in 1971
by Praeger Publishers, Inc., 111 Fourth Avenue,
New York, N.Y. 10003

Library of Congress Catalog Card Number: 71–165530

Printed in Great Britain

Contents

Illustrations

CHAPTER ONE

Carlton House

Regency London was the gayest, the most opulent and the most fashionable city in Europe. It had vigour, liveliness and style. The streets in the West End in the Season were crowded with elegant carriages: stanhopes as high as a first-floor window, tilburies, curricles, tandems, tim-whiskies and phaetons, drawn by superbly glossy, thoroughbred horses. In St James's and Piccadilly, the dandies strolled up and down, impeccably dressed in their skin-tight 'trowsers' and high 'starchers', going to White's or to Watier's to play at faro, whist and hazard. In the leafy glades of Hyde Park, the high-bred ladies of the *ton* and the high-priced and pretty demi-reps of the town drove out at the fashionable hour of five, and later in the evening both were to be seen with plumes in their hair, coquetting in the boxes at the Royal Italian Opera House in the Haymarket. Catalani, Bianchi and Naldi were singing at the Opera; Edmund Kean was acting at Drury Lane; Lord Byron dining on vinegar and potatoes with Samuel Rogers in St James's Place; Keats walking from Hampstead across the fields to Lisson Grove to visit the painter Benjamin Robert Haydon. And the Prince Regent himself (*Fig. 1*), that 'most extraordinary compound of talent, wit, buffoonery, obstinacy and good feeling', might have been found drinking cherry brandy in the overheated drawing-room of Carlton House, or closeted with his favourite architect, John Nash, discussing some new and grandiose building scheme to transform London into a city worthy to rank with the splendour of Imperial Rome.

The actual Regency was a short period—from 1811 when George Augustus, Prince of Wales, was designated Prince Regent, until 1820 when he succeeded his old, mad father as King George IV. But the dominating influence of the Prince and the style of architecture he

Fig. 1 *The Prince Regent by Robert Cruikshank* (Victoria and Albert Museum)

encouraged, which had so great an effect on the appearance of London, originated some years earlier and lasted beyond his death in 1830, through the reign of his brother King William IV into the first years of the young Queen Victoria. It was an opulent style. It had nothing of the delicate modelling and ornamentation of Robert Adam and little of the Palladian solidity of Sir William Chambers, the two leading architects of the previous generation. Yet it was based on traditional principles and its neo-Classical form with Greek pediments and porticoes, colonnades in the Doric, Ionic and Corinthian order, gigantic statuary and handsome reliefs, was an expression of the taste of the wealthy upper classes with money to burn and the bold belief that the British nation was second to none. At its best it was glorious, and it gave London many of its most superb townscapes and individual buildings; at its worst it could be empty and rather vulgar and was sometimes vitiated by the mixture of florid Egyptian ornaments, and Chinese and Gothic embellishments that were added later. But with all this, it was an English style, conceived with vision and imagination, and a style that still has an enduring aesthetic significance in the long history of London.

For the Prince the creation of a new aesthetic taste in art and architecture was an emotional release from the sobriety and the common sense of the eighteenth century. When he broke away from the dullness and the decorum of his father's Court at the age of twenty-one and took up his residence at Carlton House in 1783, he was determined to show his independence. Too much Teutonic discipline, too close a surveillance of his conduct as a youth, had made him resentful and eager to throw off the restrictions imposed by his royal upbringing. He was, moreover, a very handsome young man, with a high colour, bright blue eyes, an elegant figure and shapely legs; and the House of Hanover, with its hereditary streak of insanity, coarseness and stupidity, had never until now produced a prince with such polished manners, so much charm and such intelligence. If his uninhibited lust for music and dancing and amorous adventure, combined with the strain of being constantly in the public eye, all contributed towards the end of his life to turn him into a figure of inglorious fun for the vicious cartoonists of the 1820s, that was scarcely his fault. He was born to be extravagant in everything he did, and he was born an artist *manqué*, whose only compensation was the power and the privilege he enjoyed in patronizing the arts with a princely generosity. When he was old and ill and the Duke of Wellington refused to grant him any more money for the improvements he

3

was making at Buckingham Palace, he could still write scathingly: 'Mr Nash has been most infamously used. If those who go through the furnace for me and for my service are not protected, the favour of the Sovereign becomes worse than nugatory'—and he meant it. He would stand no nonsense—not even from Wellington—and none from the philistine House of Commons, forever carping at him and criticizing his expenditure. Economy was not a word he understood.

Carlton House in 1783 was a plain brick building in Pall Mall, standing on the site which is now covered by Waterloo Place and the Duke of York's Column. Formerly the town house of Lord Carlton, it had passed into royal ownership earlier in the eighteenth century and was a hotch-potch of old-fashioned bits and pieces. The situation overlooking St James's Park was delightful, the accommodation hardly fit for a prince wishing to surround himself with the dignity and the splendour of his high position. Unlike his father, whose interest in art was confined to the music of Handel, he had his own ideas, his own vision of the kind of palace he would like to inhabit; all he needed was the right architect to assist him. Probably his most intimate friend at this time, Charles James Fox, the brilliant spokes-man of the Whig Opposition in Parliament, brought Henry Holland to his notice in 1787, and the collaboration worked, in spite of the Prince's maddening habit of changing his mind and continually overrunning the original estimates of the alterations to be put in hand.

Holland—the son of a builder and the son-in-law of 'Capability' Brown, the famous landscape gardener of the 1760s—was a highly gifted architect, working in the classical tradition. He had already designed the new premises in St James's Street for Brooks's Club, a temple dedicated to gambling, where the rich lords of the Whig aristocracy spent their days and nights at the green baize tables. With its Corinthian pilasters and cornice, the façade was handsome and well-proportioned—as it still is today; and the spacious gaming-room or drawing-room, which has suffered very little alteration, showed the same restraint in its ornamentation and careful handling of detail. Carlton House, however, posed a much more difficult problem in the renewal and conversion of the existing buildings to the high standard demanded by a prince whose instructions were never the same for two minutes together and whose purse was by no means so fat as it seemed.

Holland began by rebuilding the Pall Mall façade in lightly rustic-ated stone, with a wide classical portico of six Corinthian columns in

Fig. 2 *Carlton House. The Ionic screen on Pall Mall designed by Henry Holland. By Ackermann, 1809* (Mansell Collection)

the centre. Then, to screen the Palace from the street, he designed a long colonnade of coupled Ionic columns with two imposing gateways (*Fig. 2*), drawing his inspiration from the recently completed Hôtel de Salm in Paris (now known as the Hôtel de la Légion d'Honneur). Londoners, apparently, found this idea odd and rather amusing; but the Parisian influence was also to be seen in the interior of the Palace with its octagon-shaped hall and handsome double staircase covered by two semi-domes meeting a coffered barrel in the centre. Horace Walpole, a lifelong connoisseur of the arts and by then a man of seventy who was not often easily pleased, was deeply impressed with the style of the interior. 'There is an august simplicity, which astonished me,' he wrote in a letter to the Countess of Upper Ossory. 'You cannot call it magnificent; it is the taste and the propriety that strike. Every ornament is at a proper distance, and none too large, but all delicate and new.' And not being an admirer of Adam's later work, he added: 'How sick we shall be after this chaste palace of Mr Adam's gingerbread and sippets of embroidery!'

Holland's individuality of style certainly owed very little to Adam, though he had the same capacity for attending to every detail of the furnishings and the decoration within the Prince's palace; and by employing a team of cabinet-makers, gilders, brass and ormolu

5

workers, both French and English, he obtained a marvellous and harmonious effect throughout all the principal apartments. Most of his decorative work was swept away when the Prince persuaded Nash some years later to remodel the interior in a more florid style, and the whole house was demolished in 1826 when, as George IV, he decided to move to Buckingham Palace. For the moment, however, free to please himself and unconcerned about the cost of the alterations, the Prince was happy enough with his London residence.

It was in the very centre of the fashionable world. Pall Mall, St James's Street (*Fig. 3*), Piccadilly and Bond Street were the main arteries of this small, exclusive coterie of the *beau monde*, the surrounding streets and squares of Mayfair their habitation. Fox lived in Arlington Street, Dick Sheridan and his lovely wife in Bruton Street, and the chandeliers blazed with light at Devonshire House in Piccadilly, where the glamorous young Duchess led the rich, the idle and the gay in dancing, gambling and gossiping into the small hours of the morning. The Prince, secretly married to the charming Mrs Fitzherbert in 1785 and officially married to the odious Princess Caroline of Brunswick eight years later, did not have far to go from Carlton House for his entertainment. At this stage he was probably quite unaware of the rest of London, except as a background to the egocentric life of pleasure he enjoyed among his chosen friends.

Had he studied Horwood's *Plan of the Cities of London and Westminster* (see pp. ii–iii) when it was published in 1794 and compared it with Rocque's map of 1746, he would have discovered the amazing growth of London in the years between. On Rocque's map there were two old and four new residential squares in the West End; Soho Square and St James's Square were planned in the seventeenth century; Hanover, Berkeley, Grosvenor and Cavendish Squares were all new and surrounded by open spaces, with the Oxford Road (later Oxford Street) as the northern boundary and Tyburn Lane (now Park Lane) running from north to south along the edge of Hyde Park. Fifty years later when Horwood's map appeared, the Portman and Harley-Cavendish Estates, laid out in a formal rectangular pattern of streets with terraced brick houses, had covered the fields and the Pleasure Gardens of Marylebone, surrounding the old village with a totally new urban development. Portman Square, begun in 1761 and Manchester Square in 1776, were both inhabited by wealthy residents, and the northern boundary of the built-up area had moved to the New Road (now the Marylebone–Euston Ring Road) running from Paddington to Islington.

Fig. 3 *St James's Street in 1800. Brooks's Club on the right, Boodle's on the left. By J. Malton* (Hulton Picture Library)

This New Road was conceived in 1757 as one of the first large-scale 'Metropolitan Improvements', its chief purpose being to canalize the herds of live sheep and cattle being driven into Smithfield Market from the western and the eastern counties in the hope of reducing the appalling confusion they caused among the rest of the traffic in the central areas. Houses were permitted on either side of the New Road only if they stood fifty feet away from it, the length of their front gardens giving them 'a most pleasing and picturesque appearance' according to T. Smith, the early nineteenth century historian of Marylebone, besides offering our modern road engineers one of the easiest stretches of road-widening in the capital, some of the gardens having survived until 1959 when Castrol House was built.

North of the New Road at the time of Horwood's map, except for Dorset Square and Mr Lord's first Cricket Ground, there were open fields and farms attached to the ancient Manor of Lisson Green, pasture-lands and osier beds bordering the little streams that trickled

7

down from the heights of Hampstead into Tyburn River; and farther towards the east, in Marylebone Park, a solitary public house called The Jew's Harp, where there was a bowling-green and a skittle-alley and much merrymaking. Eastwards again, before the New Road reached Islington, there were large patches of open ground on its south side between the Foundling Hospital, the Duke of Bedford's Bloomsbury Estate and Clerkenwell; while on the north side, fields and farmland still surrounded the newly built-up area of Somers Town, the suitably isolated Smallpox Hospital outside St Pancras village and the semi-industrialized region of Pentonville. Here and at Islington there were brick kilns and lead factories which supplied some of the building needs of the expanding metropolis, as well as dairy farms and the chalybeate wells and springs, which had once made Sadler's Wells and Islington Spa as fashionable as Bath or Tunbridge Wells. Beyond Islington, where the New Road ended, were more fields and the neglected villas of Hackney, which had once been inhabited by the rich merchants of the seventeenth century and had now declined into tenements overrun by the poor.

London south of the river showed a similar emptiness, though of a less salubrious character. Much of the land was marshy and sour, and access to it for more than five hundred years was provided only by London Bridge and the quarrelsome Thames watermen. The opening of Westminster Bridge in 1750 and the building of Black-friars in 1769 improved communications without increasing the residential areas to any great extent, except round Kennington Common. Southwark was a huddle of ancient houses and inns, with the Marshalsea Prison for debtors, the Mint, Guy's Hospital and Barclay's Brewery, which had formerly belonged to Johnson's friend, Henry Thrale, in the midst of them. Bermondsey stank of tanning factories and glue factories. Tumbledown wharves, stairs and maritime basins lined both sides of the river through Rotherhithe, Stepney, Wapping and Deptford as far as the great seventeenth and eighteenth century complex of buildings at Greenwich, where a better class residential area began and extended towards Blackheath. But the division between polite society north of the river and middle or lower class society south of it, between rich and poor in the West End and the East End, was already distinct.

Prosperous members of the middle classes—the professional men, successful doctors, lawyers, city merchants and shopkeepers of all kinds—tended to settle in the new estates north of the river; not only in Bloomsbury and the region of Marylebone, but south of Hyde

Park, where Henry Holland in 1780 developed a huge parcel of land beyond the village of Knightsbridge, which he called Hans Town after the name of the original landowner, Sir Hans Sloane. Not much of this development, beyond a few odd houses in Sloane Street and Cadogan Place, can now be seen; but for Holland it was a highly successful speculation and for the new residents, such as Jane Austen's brother Henry and his wife, a delightful situation close to the market gardens and orchards of Brompton and not far from the village of Chelsea, where there were coffee houses, taverns and other rural haunts of pleasure.

Ranelagh Gardens in Chelsea, so fashionable with the *beau monde* in the middle of the eighteenth century, closed down for lack of funds in 1805. Vauxhall, across the river, maintained its popularity for longer and was often visited by the young Prince of Wales, whose affability and condescension charmed the other visitors. On masquerade nights, which were more expensive than ordinary nights, the gardens were illuminated with a thousand lamps, 'so disposed that they all take fire together', and the company wandered down the long avenues of trees admiring the fountains, the cascades and Roubiliac's fine statue of Mr Handel, or listened to the musicians playing in the orchestra pavilion (*Fig. 4*), before supping on Arrack punch, powdered beef, custards and syllabubs laced with wine in one of the small supper boxes arranged in the leafy arbours. A good deal of 'squealing and squalling' went on among the young ladies venturing alone into the Dark Walk, where impudent young gentlemen hovered about, waiting to pursue them. But Vauxhall was fun on a fine summer's evening and it was a sad day when Victorian respectability and commercial greed did away with the Pleasure Gardens in 1859.

Respectability was not yet a very highly prized virtue among the rich or the poor in London; law and order were not easily maintained in a city which had grown so rapidly. The watchmen or 'Charlies' were often corrupt and incapable of coping with the disorderly persons who roved round the streets at night looking for trouble. Fielding's Bow Street Runners, though more reliable, were few in number, and it was not until the last year of George IV's reign that Sir Robert Peel established the Metropolitan Police Force at Scotland Yard. There were thieves, pickpockets, footpads, highwaymen and confidence tricksters everywhere, and it was dangerous to travel beyond the turnpike at Hyde Park Corner through Knightsbridge after dark. The conceited 'Macaronis', young bucks and blades of

9

Fig. 4 *Vauxhall Pleasure Gardens in 1785. By Rowlandson*
(Mansell Collection)

the town, were no less vicious in their behaviour than the prostitutes they pursued around the brothels of Covent Garden or the criminal underworld that fed on their dissipations. An affray could break out anywhere at any time and be settled with bare fists in the street, or lead to a more serious riot with everyone joining in the general scrimmage while the 'Charlies' made haste to save their own skins by disappearing. Duelling was against the law and gradually dying out, but a very high proportion of Englishmen in the Regency positively enjoyed fighting each other on the slightest pretext and the amount of liquor they habitually consumed made them hot-tempered and rampageous.

They had an enormous lust for life and their energy was phenomenal. Fox once gambled at Brooks's (*Fig. 5*) without a break from eight o'clock in the evening until three o'clock the following afternoon; then, with his wits unimpaired by lack of sleep, he delivered a long speech in the House of Commons on the Thirty-Nine Articles, before returning to Brooks's for dinner at eleven-thirty. From there he went on to White's for another session at the gaming tables lasting until seven o'clock in the morning, only giving himself time for a quick nap, before he set out for the races at Newmarket. One minute he was £10 or £20,000 up and the next £15 or £30,000 down without turning a hair or showing any sign of emotion; and he called his ante-room in Arlington Street 'the Jerusalem Chamber' from the number of Jewish moneylenders he entertained there to provide him with the ready cash to return again to the tables and try his luck once more. Yet with all his extravagance and his insane passion for gambling, Fox was a statesman of the highest integrity with the widest possible knowledge of his country's affairs, a classical scholar, a sportsman and a man whose word could be trusted. As a close intimate of the young Prince of Wales his experience was valuable. As a figure on the London scene, he represented the old century and the new, the wit, the gaiety, the fashion and the frivolity of Mayfair and the basic vitality of the nation's flourishing capital.

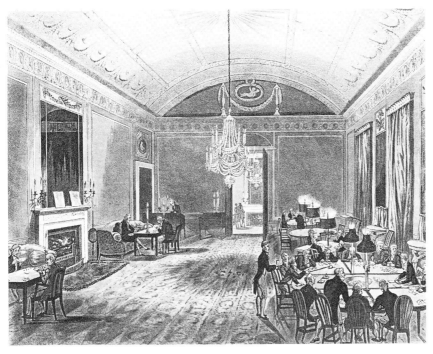

Fig. 5 *Brooks's Club. By Rowlandson and Pugin, 1808* (Mansell Collection)

CHAPTER TWO

The Mercantile City

The fashionable gentlemen of Mayfair seldom penetrated into the City. Indeed, when Beau Brummell once met Sheridan in the Strand, he loftily asserted that he had lost his way by straying so far east of Piccadilly—and the Strand was only the connecting link between the new West End and the very old, historic centre of London.

The City had not changed much since the rebuilding after the Great Fire of 1666. Wren's great dome of St Paul's and the marvellous spires of his fifty-one churches dominated the skyline above the roofs and chimney-pots of the new brick houses. Within the irregular boundary of the old Roman and medieval wall, the ancient pattern of the streets persisted. Cheapside, Cornhill, Gracechurch Street and Fenchurch Street, the scene of Queen Elizabeth I's royal progress and of King Charles II's entry into London after the Restoration, were the major highways, together with the narrower streets radiating from the centre towards the eight city gateways. All these—Cripplegate, Ludgate, Aldgate, Aldersgate, Moorgate, Bishopsgate and Bridgegate—were demolished in 1760 to give the ever-increasing wheeled traffic in and out of the City more room to move; only Temple Bar between Fleet Street and the Strand remained for another hundred years, until that too was taken down and the present memorial erected.

The government of the City—then as now—was vested in the Lord Mayor, the Aldermen and the Sheriffs, drawn from members of the old-established Livery Companies, and was independent of the Crown and Parliament. Their Council Hall and Court of Assembly were in the fifteenth-century Guildhall, which was partially rebuilt in 1788 by George Dance, the Younger, who followed his father as Clerk of the Works to the City Corporation. The architect also of Newgate Prison, a massive and solid structure that survived until 1902 on the site of the Old Bailey, Dance attempted a Gothic fantasy for the façade of the Guildhall, which can still be seen, though horribly over-exposed by the recent destruction of the Georgian Court House beside it. A new road, King Street, and the widening of an ancient lane into Queen Street gave direct access from the Guildhall to the Thames waterfront at a point where John Rennie was to build the first Southwark Bridge in 1815.

But the heart of the mercantile City was—as it still is—at the intersection of the Poultry, a continuation of Cheapside, with Corn-hill, Lombard Street and Threadneedle Street. Here, the Mansion House, the Royal Exchange and the Bank of England occupy three sides of a triangular space, which from the time of the first Royal Exchange built by Sir Thomas Gresham in 1566 was the crowded meeting-place of the City merchants. Gresham's Exchange was destroyed in the Great Fire and rebuilt in a handsome style in 1667, serving its purpose until it also was burnt to the ground in 1838 and replaced by the present building designed by William Tite. The Mansion House, with its ceremonial staircase and pillared balcony behind the classical portico, was designed by George Dance, the Elder, in 1734 as the official residence of the Lord Mayor, and its vast Egyptian Hall, which has changed very little, was a suitable setting for civic receptions as the accumulated wealth of the City increased through the eighteenth century and spilled over into the nineteenth. The Bank of England was a comparatively small cluster of buildings until 1788 when John Soane, at the age of thirty-five, was appointed its architect in succession to Sir Robert Taylor.

Soane—knighted somewhat belatedly in 1831—was the son of a small builder in Reading. He worked in the office of the younger Dance and then for Henry Holland, won the Silver and Gold Medals at the Royal Academy and a travelling scholarship which enabled him to go to Italy. In Rome he met the Italian artist Piranezi and some of the English *cognoscenti* residing there, among them Thomas Pitt, a cousin of the Prime Minister, and the 4th Earl of Bristol. The patronage he was promised by the eccentric Earl-Bishop came to nothing, but the influence of Thomas Pitt with the Prime Minister eventually secured him the appointment to the Bank of England, and this great task of remodelling and rebuilding the biggest financial house in the world absorbed all his time and energy for the next forty-five years.

The governors of the Bank gave Soane a free hand. Even the out-break of the war with France which went on for over twenty years,

Fig. 6 *Interior of the Bank of England. Drawing by Soane*
(Mansell Collection)

did not deter them; for the war itself and England's policy of granting
big loans to her allies increased the business of the Bank and emphasized the need of creating proper facilities for its smooth functioning.
Soane built the various courts (*Fig. 6*)—the Bank Stock Office, the
Lothbury Court with its triumphal arch and Corinthian screens,
the Governor's Court and the Five Pound Note Office—with a view
to their use in the daily business of the Bank, but with a sensational
breadth of imagination and a monumental grandeur. On the outside,
he enveloped the whole site with a screen wall in the stylized order
of the Temple of Vesta at Tivoli, completing it with the rounded
'Tivoli Corner' where Princes Street runs into Lothbury (*Fig. 7*).

Insensitive rebuilding of the Bank in the 1920s, although retaining
Soane's screen wall, has destroyed the balance of his greatest achievement. He was a dedicated artist, totally absorbed in his work and
continually bent on exploring the ultimate possibilities of architectural
experiment. At the Royal Hospital in Chelsea he built a functional
gateway to the stables in plain London brick with no ornament at all,
but in scale and proportion a masterpiece of abstract design. At No.
13 Lincoln's Inn Fields, the town house he built himself in 1812 (now

the Soane Museum), he let his imagination run wild in a totally opposite direction, creating a fantastic Piranezian setting for his enormous collection of statuary, plaster casts, archaeological fragments, paintings and *objets d'art*. Indeed, the Monk's Parlour, the Dome, the Crypt, the Breakfast Room and the Picture Room with its folding panels revealing more and more pictures and drawings one behind the other, have a strange, hectic intensity, a disturbing sense of fanaticism and of a brilliant mind on the very edge of disaster. Soane apparently suffered from neurotic fits of depression and perhaps his 'feverish fancies' as they were called by his friends, found expression here, in his own home, in contrast to his more disciplined work at the Bank and elsewhere.

The Bank was the only major public building to be erected in the City in the years between 1793 and 1815; all other large undertakings were postponed by the exigencies of the war with France. Not that despondency was ever the mood of the City, even in the darkest years when England stood alone and Napoleon's conquests encompassed the whole of Europe. Provided England had command of the seas, and this was finally assured by Lord Nelson's victory at Trafalgar

Fig. 7 *Bank of England. By T. H. Shepherd, 1827* (Mansell Collection)

in 1805, her trading round the world did not suffer. In fact there was more trade, not less; and while news of the victory at Trafalgar set all the bells of the City tolling, the clerks of the East India Office in Leadenhall Street, one of whom was Charles Lamb, were patiently recording in their dusty ledgers the arrival of the company's rich cargoes from abroad.

Most of the City's business, however, with the exception of one or two very large and old-established companies, was not transacted in a formal office at all; it was done in the coffee houses, which ever since the middle of the seventeenth century had flourished in the warren of narrow courts and alleys around the Royal Exchange. In spite of the Blitz and the tasteless post-war modernization of the City, it is still possible (though it may not be for long) to trace the pattern of the old courts and alleys behind St Michael's Church, Cornhill, where Jonathen's, Garraway's, Lloyd's, the Jamaica and the Jerusalem Coffee Houses thrived on the custom of the eighteenth and early nineteenth century merchants.

'The Vertue of the COFFEE Drink', according to one of the earliest advertisements, apart from it being 'an excellent Cure for the Spleen and the Dropsy', was that it 'prevented Drowsiness' and made a man 'fit for business', and the coffee houses themselves were run on democratic lines. Anyone on the payment of one penny at the bar could take a seat and smoke his pipe in comfort, read the news-papers free of charge and join in the conversation or not, according to his inclination. Traders of all descriptions used the coffee houses as a business address and found them a convenient meeting place where they could discuss their affairs with other merchants sharing the same interests; and the coffee house proprietors rendered them all kinds of services, handling their correspondence, advertising thefts and rewards, arranging passages on ships bound for the West Indies, Turkey and the Far East and conducting auction sales 'by Inch of Candle', the last bid before the candle flame went out securing the lot for sale.

Garraway's, originally in Sweeting's Rents and afterwards in Exchange Alley, was frequented by the most prominent auctioneers and brokers in merchandise. The sales there covered a variety of commodities such as sugar, Spanish tobacco, indigo, ivory, Jamaica rum, timber, textiles, 'damaged rice' and other salvaged goods, as well as property, including 'a Capital Plantation in the Island of Grenada and the negroes on the Plantation amounting to about 100', leasehold and freehold estates in London and the country, insurance policies and 'a genteel dwelling-house at Ham Common'. Competition from the splendid New Auction Mart built in 1810 behind the Bank at the corner of Throgmorton Street and Bartholomew Lane at a cost of £40,000, did not diminish the prestige of Garraway's. Sales continued to be held in their old-fashioned premises until 1866 when the site was taken over by Martin's Bank.

Jonathen's, on the opposite side of Exchange Alley, was the resort of the stockbrokers and stock-jobbers all through the eighteenth century, but by 1800 had become the Stock Exchange Coffee House in Threadneedle Street, where 'excellent dinners at a reasonable price' were to be had 'every afternoon' and 'beds procured'. Edward Cooper, a Wine and Brandy Merchant, who also kept the Bell Inn at Shooter's Hill, was the energetic proprietor responsible for the management of the coffee house at this time; but before long, as the volume of business in stocks and shares expanded, most of his regular clients, paying a subscription of 6d. a day, began to trade in the new Stock Exchange opened in 1802 in Capel Court, on the site of the immense new tower of the modern Stock Exchange.

The business of Lloyd's, as the principal centre for everyone concerned with traffic on the high seas, had also developed from the association of traders meeting in the first coffee house of that name by Tower Hill. Afterwards Lloyd's had moved to Lombard Street and then to Pope's Head Alley, before becoming established in 1774 'over the North West Corner of the Royal Exchange'. Merchants, underwriters, insurance brokers, sea-captains and shipowners with agents all over the world gathered in the first-floor room above the Exchange; and in 1799 the Lutine Bell, salvaged from a frigate of that name which was wrecked with all hands aboard and a cargo of bullion, was installed there, one stroke of its great hammer announcing that a vessel was missing at sea and two strokes that she was safe after all. *Lloyd's List*—then, as now—was the most accurate publication dealing with every detail of maritime news, and the men who traded there had a high reputation for the honesty and integrity of their business methods.

During the Napoleonic Wars, subscriptions running into large figures were raised at Lloyd's for the relief of the widows and orphans of the fighting seamen who lost their lives. Patriotic fervour ran high. Napoleon's gibe at 'the nation of shopkeepers' was treated as a joke or with contempt, though it was not without some truth. Shopkeeping in its widest sense was a major source of income for the inhabitants of the City. It signified the wholesale and the retail trade, as well as the actual fashioning of the goods for sale by the master craftsmen and the journeymen and apprentices they employed. Booksellers were printers and publishers of the books and pamphlets they sold, shoemakers, hatters and tailors had workshops behind the premises they occupied, bakers and pastrycooks were enveloped in the hot floury smell of baking bread and mutton pies from the huge ovens they stoked all day and night. In the one small area between Cornhill and Lombard Street, bounded by St Michael's Alley and Exchange Alley, there were over forty different shops, packed in together like a child's box of bricks. Eight of them were booksellers and stationers, six of them woollen-drapers, haberdashers and hosiers, four of them tallow-chandlers, oilmen and hardwaremen, three of them hatters, two of them cabinet-makers, one a pewterer, others a toyman, a sword cutler, a button-maker and a music shop. There were also half a dozen attorneys' and insurance offices, one Gunpowder Office and a great many barbers, the only tradesmen, beside the pawnbrokers, who were allowed to retain their decorative poles after 1762 when the numbering of houses was enforced and the overhanging shop signs everywhere were ordered to be removed.

Both within the City and outside it, shopkeeping covered the widest possible area. A guidebook for visitors called *The Picture of London*, published in 1803, described: 'Two sets of streets running nearly parallel, almost from the Eastern extremity of the town to the Western, forming (with the exception of a very few houses) a line of shops. One, lying to the South, nearer the river, extends from Mile End to Parliament Street, including Whitechapel, Leadenhall Street, Cornhill, Cheapside, St Paul's Churchyard, Ludgate Street, Fleet Street, the Strand and Charing Cross. The other, to the North, reaches from Shoreditch Church almost to the end of Oxford Street, including Shoreditch, Bishopsgate Street, Threadneedle Street, Cheapside, Newgate Street, Snow-hill, Holborn, Broad Street, St Giles and Oxford Street. The Southern line, which is the most splendid, is more than three miles in length, and the other about four miles,' the writer noted; and assuming that the visitor was not already utterly bewildered by the multiplicity of goods to be found from one end of London to the other, he went on to describe the shops in Gracechurch Street and Fenchurch Street and the high quality of the merchandise to be seen in the most fashionable shops of all 'at the West end of the town'.

By this time most of the rich merchants had moved out of the City into the more salubrious air of Bloomsbury and Islington, or even as far as Epping; but the small shopkeepers continued to live over their place of business, their wives and children helping them with their work and their apprentices often sharing the cramped conditions above or below stairs. And in spite of long hours, congested work-rooms and the often cantankerous relationship between the young apprentice and his master, there was plenty of opportunity for anyone with intelligence, persistence and courage to make good. Ambitious young men from all over the country came to London to seek their fortune in trade, and many of them were successful, like William Cook, who arrived in 1806 and began with a small outfitters in Clerkenwell, before moving to larger premises in Cheapside and finally being elected to the Worshipful Company of Drapers in 1822.

Different trades belonged to different areas. St Paul's Churchyard was the heart of the drapery trade and of the booksellers; Clerkenwell was noted for the watchmakers, jewellers and goldsmiths working there; Whitechapel for its tailoring and Spitalfields, ever since the Huguenots had settled there, for its silk weaving. The markets inside and outside the City were also clearly defined: Billingsgate, the oldest, alive with wet fish and salt fish and the riotous, rawboned fishwives in leather aprons and scarlet petticoats; Smithfield, by the historic church of St Bartholomew the Great and the equally historic hospital founded by the saintly Prior Rahere, seething and stinking with live cattle and sheep driven in from the countryside; Covent Garden, a mixture of brothels and taverns, and fruit and vegetables piled high on the stalls leaning against Inigo Jones's once fashionable Piazza; Spitalfields in the East End and the Borough at the Southwark end of London Bridge, supplied by the huge old Kentish wagons lumbering up the High Street and the slow moving barges on the river.

All this shopkeeping and marketing, however, was only the visible tip of the City's trade, which extended round the world beyond the seas. London's river was packed with ocean-going sailing ships: huge East Indiamen, tea clippers, galliots, whalers, schooners and hundreds of smaller vessels. The value of exports and imports to the Pool below London Bridge had doubled in ten years and by 1800 was calculated to be in the region of £70,000,000. The delays in unloading the heavy cargoes of wine and sugar, tea and coffee, timber, ivory, raw silk and other such goods, were appalling. The so-called system of 'legal quays', which had suited the ways of the eighteenth century, was now totally inadequate and the amount of smuggling and organized plunder that went on from the open quays and unguarded wharves along the river banks resulted in a serious loss of merchandise to all

Fig. 8 *West India Dock. By T. H. Shepherd, 1827* (Mansell Collection)

the companies concerned. Something had to be done, war or no war; indeed, because the war had increased the volume of trade beyond all expectations. And so the City had to give way to parliamentary pressure and in conjunction with various joint stock companies, to begin on the great dock-building programme, which went on for more than twenty years and was the greatest triumph of engineering the world had yet seen.

The West India Dock (*Fig. 8*) in the Isle of Dogs was the first undertaking, built by Ralph Walker and John Rennie, whose great block of brick warehouses, designed with a splendid simplicity, stood between the two rectangular import and export basins, which were big enough to hold vessels of more than 750 tons. The London Dock at Wapping was begun two years later by Daniel Alexander, the architect of Maidstone Gaol, and finished in 1805 at a cost of £2,000,000. The East India Dock (1806) and the Surrey Docks (1807) followed, the entrance to the East India guarded by the great granite portal designed by Rennie, which has survived in a reconstructed form, and much of the work being done by the new steam-powered engines for pumping water, pile driving and grinding mortar. Then there was a pause until 1825, when 1,250 houses and 11,300 inhabitants, together with the medieval buildings of St Katherine's Hospital, were removed from the Georgian slum area east of the Tower of London to make room for St Katherine's Dock, covering an area of twenty-four acres. The famous Scottish road engineer, Thomas Telford, was responsible for the layout of the dockyard and Philip Hardwick for the brown brick warehouses with their noble Doric columns of granite, which give great dignity to this early example of functional design serving a commercial purpose.

The future of the early nineteenth century docks is now very uncertain as the modern Port of London continues to be moved farther towards the mouth of the Thames. But at the time of their building they were among the wonders of the world. Prince Pückler-Muskau, a German visitor to England in 1826, admired them almost more than anything else he saw. He called the West India Dock and warehouses 'an immeasurable work, at the sight of which the most cold-blooded spectator must feel astonishment, and a sort of awe at the greatness and the might of England. What a capital lies here in buildings, wares and vessels!' he exclaimed, and he went on to describe the tall warehouses, where 'there was sugar enough to sweeten the whole adjoining basin and rum enough to make half England drunk'. He learnt that over two thousand artisans and overseers were employed daily in the dockyard and he was impressed by the number of well-contrived hoists and machines used to unload the vessels moored in the basin. 'I looked on . . . while blocks of mahogany and other foreign woods, many larger than the largest oak, were lifted up like feathers and deposited on drays or waggons as carefully as if they had been brittle ware,' he wrote, adding: 'Everything is on a colossal scale. . . . But I was obliged to leave this interesting place sooner than I wished, as the entrance gate and all the warehouses are closed by 4 o'clock, and the gatekeeper very coolly assured me that if the King were there, he would not wait a minute!'

Nothing, in fact, could now stand in the way of commercial progress—not even royalty itself. St Katherine's Dock in the very shadow of the great fortress built by William the Conqueror to overawe the City, was a symbol of the historic development of London from the Norman Conquest onwards towards its destiny as the capital of a great mercantile nation. The moated Tower with its 'blood boltered' history, though still sometimes used as a prison for political offenders, was already little more than a tourist attraction. It housed the Royal

Menagerie until 1834, the Royal Armoury and the Crown Jewels, which were kept in an old smoky cupboard in one of the vaults, dimly lit by two tallow candles and shown to visitors by an ancient harridan of the most ungainly appearance. The ravens croaked on the Green and the Yeomen Warders or 'Beefeaters' in their Tudor uniforms stood on guard, but no one any longer travelled by water to the Traitors' Gate and the last public execution on Tower Hill had taken place in 1747.

Not far from where the scaffold had stood, on the east side of the Hill, another symbol of national prosperity was built in 1810 by John Johnson and the twenty-eight-year-old Robert Smirke. This was the new Royal Mint (in use until 1969), one of Smirke's first essays in designing a large building in the classical manner with breadth and simplicity, if not with any very outstanding originality. Much younger than Nash or Soane, with whom he had studied as a boy, Smirke was so successful, he was appointed with the two older and more experienced architects to the Board of Works in 1815 and as time went on was responsible for a number of public buildings

Fig. 9 *Entrance to the Regent's Canal at Limehouse. By T. H. Shepherd, 1827* (Mansell Collection)

commissioned by the City and the Government. These included the old Custom House adjoining Billingsgate Market, which had been destroyed by fire in 1813 and rebuilt by another pupil of Soane's, David Laing, but owing to some miscalculation on his part had begun to subside when Smirke was called in, either to repair the damage or to start again. In fact, he demolished the centre portion of Laing's building altogether and in 1825 rebuilt the whole of the river frontage in one of his most pleasing designs, with the graceful Ionic columns and elegant proportions that can still be enjoyed by anyone travelling on a boat down the river.

The importance of the river as a highway for commercial transport and the feasibility of linking the new docks with the inland waterways built in the eighteenth century, encouraged John Nash early in the Regency to plan the construction of the Regent's Canal as a means of joining up the Grand Junction Canal from the expanding industrial centres of the Midlands with the Thames at Regent's Canal Dock (*Fig. 9*) at Limehouse. A company formed in 1812 authorized the work on this bold idea to begin and though lack of funds at one time almost brought the whole project to grief and plunged Nash himself into deep waters financially, the Canal was finished at last in 1820, when the formal opening took place and was celebrated by an aquatic procession of boats, ornamented with flags and streamers and filled with ladies and gentlemen thoughtfully provided with refreshments and wine.

The new waterway cut a swathe ten and a half miles long through North London, from Paddington where it met the Grand Junction Canal, round the north of the new Regent's Park, through Camden Town, Islington, Hoxton, Bethnal Green and Mile End to Limehouse; and before the coming of the railways, it was thick with gaily painted monkey-boats, hauled along by the horses walking the tow-path. Much neglected in later years when the traffic fell away and the charming houses on its banks deteriorated, the Regent's Canal is now again, in some parts, a delightful residential area—in Paddington where it is known as 'Little Venice', at Primrose Hill and in Islington —and for twentieth-century Londoners, weary of the noise and the congestion of the streets, a sudden gleam of freshness and tranquillity.

Not that London in the Regency did not suffer just as much— perhaps even more—from noise and congestion; from the ballad singers and the street pedlars, the rowdy pedestrians, the clatter of iron hoofs and iron wheels in the constant coming and going of the horses and carriages. 'Further still did we wander on in the tumultuous

23

City,' Prince Pückler-Muskau wrote, 'where you may be lost like a flitting atom, if you do not pass on the right or left according to rule; and where you seem to be in constant danger of being spitted on the shaft of a cabriolet driving too near the narrow *trottoir*, or crushed under the weight of an overloaded stage-coach.' And on another occasion when he rode into the City, his horse took fright and he was almost mobbed to death before he could get the terrified animal under control.

Not much was done to ease the flow of traffic except by the building of three new bridges across the Thames, one at Vauxhall, one at Southwark and one at the Somerset House corner of the Strand; and these were all projected and carried through as speculative ventures by private companies, not with the aid of public funds. All three were designed by the brilliant Scottish engineer and architect, John Rennie, but money ran out at Vauxhall soon after work had begun in 1811 and the bridge eventually had to be constructed in a very modified form. Waterloo, begun as Strand Bridge in the autumn of the same year and finished in 1817, was more fortunate. The company raised the colossal sum of £1,050,000 and could congratulate themselves on footing the bill for what the Italian sculptor Canova called 'the noblest bridge in the world' (*Fig. 10*).

Fig. 10 *Waterloo Bridge. By W. Westall* (Hulton Picture Library)

It was a masterpiece. Rennie's design of nine semi-elliptical arches carrying the roadway across the river in a level line was magnificent in scale. It had simplicity and a structural nobility that matched the grandeur of Somerset House and gave a superb horizontal emphasis to the river landscape as a foil to the still unravished skyline of London with its spires and pinnacles and airy domes. Moreover, the controlled harmony of the structure dictated the balance of the architectural detail and here, as in all his work, Rennie's judgment was faultless. Pairs of Doric columns on the piers supported a continuous entablature surmounted by a simple balustrade in grey Aberdeen granite; no excess of ornament or prettification was necessary. Rennie had demonstrated his genius in the complete fusion of the architect and the engineer and Waterloo Bridge (demolished 1927) was one of the glories of London.

Southwark Bridge, begun in 1815 and finished in 1819 (but demolished in 1914), posed a different problem and was an even more daring engineering feat; for the City Corporation objected to the bridge as an obstacle to river traffic and to obtain their consent, Rennie had to undertake to cross the river in three spans. This he accomplished successfully by using three cast-iron segmental arches supported by stone piers, the central arch spanning 240 feet, a distance which had never before been attempted at a single throw and would not have been possible without the new techniques in moulding iron perfected by the iron-masters in the North of England. The fixing of the arches was 'an extremely delicate and nice process, but the whole operation so adjusted that the parts remained in perfect equilibrium and not a bolt was broken'.

After Southwark, London Bridge, which had been patched and repaired down the centuries, the houses along it being removed in 1761, was the next and last commission Rennie undertook, but he did not live to see his design realized and the actual construction was completed by his son in 1831. Again it was a massive structure unadorned by any meretricious ornamentation and a triumph of engineering skill combined with great architectural quality. But now, that too has gone—sold to the Americans in 1969—and nothing remains of Rennie's stupendous achievement as the master bridge-builder of the Regency except his graceful bridge across the Serpentine in Hyde Park.

The new bridges made some difference, but not a great deal, to the flow of the traffic; for the fast roads with a hard surface developed by Telford and Macadam throughout the kingdom at the beginning of the Regency, brought more wheeled traffic than ever to the turn-pikes that were the gateway into London. From the west and the south-west, a stream of vehicles passed through the toll-gates at Notting Hill and at Hyde Park Corner. From the north, they stopped at Islington, at Highgate and at Hampstead, where the last of the toll-houses can still be seen on the Spaniards Road. And all this traffic piled up in central London, just as it does today, though with even more confusion since the streets were full of mettlesome horses, and their riders or drivers needed the utmost skill to avoid accidents. Bollards had to be provided at the street corners to stop the carriages wheeling round on to the pavement and running the pedestrians down, but everyone, rich or poor, fancied himself as a judge of horse flesh and nowhere else in the world were such splendid horses and carriages to be seen.

Speed, smartness and efficiency were the criteria of the age in private and in public transport, and the mail coaches were one of the sights of London. Twenty-seven of them, painted maroon and black with scarlet wheels and the royal coat of arms emblazoned on the doors, were drawn up in double file outside the General Post Office in Lombard Street every night of the year except Sundays; and punctually at eight o'clock they set off on their long journeys, piled high with passengers and luggage, and with the guard in his royal scarlet livery standing on the boot at the back with his feet on top of the locked mail-box, blowing his long brass horn to clear the way ahead. 'The absolute perfection of all the appointments about the carriages . . . their brilliant cleanliness and their beautiful sim-plicity' excited the fervent admiration of Thomas de Quincey, and the power of the horses, 'incarnated in their fiery eyeballs, dilated nostrils and thunder-beating hoofs', first revealed to him 'the glory of motion' when he travelled up to London as a student from Oxford, riding outside on the box by the coachman. 'We heard our speed!' he declared. 'We saw it! We felt it as thrilling!'

And behind all this wonderful display was a complex organization that never failed to function smoothly, even in fog and frost and snow. The Post Office had the monopoly of the coaches and paid the guards to look after the mail-bags and to see that every journey was kept up to schedule precisely on time; private enterprise horsed the coaches in and out of London and the two leading contractors—William Chaplin and Edward Sherman—made a fortune. Chaplin operated from the Swan with Two Necks (*Fig. 11*) in Lad Lane off Gresham Street and Sherman from the old Bull and Mouth Inn,

Fig. 11 *The Swan with Two Necks. By James Pollard* (Mansell Collection)

exactly opposite the new General Post Office in St Martins-le-Grand, another massive building designed by Smirke in 1829 (demolished 1913). Both, besides their contracts with the Post Office, ran fast long-distance day coaches to destinations as far apart as Holyhead, Bristol, Shrewsbury, Carlisle, Edinburgh, Birmingham, Exeter, Manchester and Brighton. Both were tough, hard-headed business-men, but Chaplin's methods were upright and honourable, whereas Sherman's were often rather devious and he was ready to squeeze the last ounce out of his men and his animals.

More people than ever before were travelling about in the Regency. From five o'clock in the morning until eight or nine o'clock while the day coaches were loading up and the mails and night coaches were coming in, with all their passengers, parcels and luggage, the yard at the Swan with Two Necks seethed with excitement and activity. Half-awake travellers, shaken out of their beds before dawn in the first and second floor galleries round the yard, pulled on their boots and tumbled down the stairs in the dark to take their places in the outgoing coaches, with only time enough for a nip of brandy and water. Cold and bleary-eyed travellers from the night coaches, untangled their aching limbs and hastened into the coffee room for breakfast, to feast on cold pigeon-pie, boiled beef and ham, grilled kidneys and bacon, hot buttered toast and muffins, with quantities of tea and coffee or stronger waters to sweeten their appetite. And this was going on everywhere, every day of the week, in all the numerous coaching inns all over the City and in Holborn, Aldgate, Southwark, Charing Cross and the West End.

Competition was relentless. Chaplin owned the Manchester 'Defiance' and the Birmingham 'Greyhound', but Sherman put the Manchester 'Telegraph' on the same road which went faster than the 'Defiance', and both Mrs Mountain of the Bell Inn, Aldgate, and William Horne of the Golden Cross at Charing Cross tried to monopolize the road to Birmingham with their 'Tally-Ho' coaches. Chaplin built underground stables at the Swan with Two Necks to accommodate some of the eighteen hundred horses he owned, and the number of coachmen, guards, horsekeepers, ostlers, stable-boys, storekeepers, chambermaids, porters and cooks he employed was well over two thousand. Besides the Swan with Two Necks, he owned the Spread Eagle and Cross Keys in Gracechurch Street, the White Horse in Fetter Lane, several West End offices and large stables on the outskirts of London at Hounslow, Putney and Whetstone. His business was famous throughout the kingdom; his black and red coaches were fast, reliable and superbly equipped. But the wind of change began to blow down the Great North Road in 1833 when excavations for the new railroad from Birmingham to London were started, and within a few years the railways had arrived.

One by one the coaches fell away like autumn leaves and before long the coaching inns with their crowds of spectators and passengers, their army of servants, horsekeepers and stable-boys, were deserted. Lad Lane was obliterated in the Blitz and a plaque on the wall in St Martins-le-Grand is all that remains to mark the site of the old Bull and Mouth. Only a fragment of the George Inn, Southwark, has survived, with its gallery and its cosy panelled coffee-room, to recall the splendour of the golden age of coaching and the immortal characters conceived by the very young Londoner, Charles Dickens, writing from his own first-hand experience of travelling about in the late 1820s.

Westminster and the Government

By 1800 Fleet Street and the Strand were crowded with traffic and the river was no longer, as it had been in the past, the main highway for people travelling between the cities of London and Westminster. The great palaces of the nobility with their water-gates and stairs going down to the riverfront had been demolished and the gardens behind them reaching to the Strand turned over to the developers. Robert Adam built the Adelphi in 1768 on the site of the Bishop of Durham's house, Sir William Chambers cleared away the sixteenth-century palace of the Protector Somerset to erect Somerset House in 1776; and on the north side of the Strand, Exeter House had been replaced by Exeter Hall and a row of shops, which before long were extended all the way along the street to Charing Cross.

Here, where Samuel Johnson once declared 'the full tide of human existence' was to be found, the last of the great patrician mansions, Northumberland House, still stood (demolished 1874), its Jacobean grandeur somewhat diminished by the crowd of little shops coming right up to its façade. Opposite was the Golden Cross, a famous and flourishing coaching inn, owned by William Horne and his son, Benjamin Worthy Horne, who ran a service of fast day coaches to Brighton, travelling at twelve miles an hour and reaching the fashionable seaside resort in less than five hours. Behind the yard of the Golden Cross, a cluster of small and rather shabby little eighteenth-century houses hemmed in the church of St Martin-in-the-Fields and the entrance to the Royal Mews; while beyond the Mews, Cockspur Street led into Pall Mall and the Haymarket, where the enormous country wagons filled with bales of straw and fodder for London's innumerable horses caused havoc among the smart equipages of the gentry visiting the Little Theatre, the Italian Opera

29

D

Fig. 12 *Melbourne House, originally remodelled by Henry Holland for the Duke of York* (Hulton Picture Library)

House and Fribourg & Treyer's shop 'on the pavement', where the finest 'Foreign Snuff, Tobacco and Oriental Segars' were for sale.

All this area was to undergo a transformation with the development of Trafalgar Square and its surroundings, though not until the late 1820s after the other 'Metropolitan Improvements' made by the most notable of all the Regency architects, John Nash. While the Prince resided at Carlton House, it remained much as it had always been, and one thing then was the same as it is now—the equestrian statue of King Charles I, re-erected to his memory in 1674, faced the length of Whitehall, where twenty-five years before he had walked to his death on the scaffold. Nothing remained of the old royal palace of the Tudors and the Stuarts except Inigo Jones's superb Banqueting House, which is still the greatest glory of Whitehall. Built in 1620 in Portland stone and on purely Palladian lines, its strict classical form exercised an enormous influence over the architects working a hundred years later in the Palladian revival promoted by Lord Burlington and his circle, especially on William Kent who designed the Guard House to the palace, now the Horse Guards, on the opposite side of Whitehall in 1751. Kent achieved a very harmonious building in the Horse Guards, worthy of its beautiful setting; and Robert Adam proved to be his equal ten years later in conceiving the delicate contrast of the screen he designed for the Admiralty farther to the north of Whitehall, while to the south of the Horse Guards, Henry Holland built the elegant portico of what is now the Scottish Office, but in the Regency was the home of Lady Melbourne, one of the most successful hostesses in high society.

This house was originally remodelled by Holland in 1788 for the Prince's younger brother, the Duke of York (*Fig. 12*), but the Duke, on returning from abroad four years later, took a fancy to Melbourne House in Piccadilly and begged his brother to sound the Melbournes out with a view to arranging a swap between them of one house with the other. Lady Melbourne, ever ambitious for her family and seeing the advantage of doing the royal brothers a favour, was not averse to the idea, while Lord Melbourne invariably did what his wife told him to do, before going off to spend the day at Brooks's and the night with his mistress. So in 1793, the Duke moved to Piccadilly and the Melbournes to Whitehall, where the gracious portico led into a circular vestibule lit by a lantern in the shallow dome above it and the painted ballroom with its windows overlooking St James's Park was redecorated for the entertainment of Lady Melbourne's distinguished guests.

Night after night the liveried footmen ushered in the most brilliant men and the most beautiful women of the privileged Whig aristocracy: the ravishing Duchess of Devonshire and her sister Lady Bessborough, with her handsome lover Lord Granville Leveson-Gower; Fox and Sheridan, both sometimes drunk but always amusing; Lord John Townsend and the Prince himself, calling late and staying to supper at the candle-lit table. Informality and respect for rank and fashion were artfully combined at the Melbourne House parties, pleasure with the absorbing and tantalizing problems of success in this, the only world that mattered, gaiety and splendour and great wealth with Lady Melbourne's overriding ambition and her talent for getting what she wanted out of life. She was beautiful and feminine, with dark eyes and a shapely figure, yet vigorous and practical, with a clear judgment that never failed to stimulate her friends or to make her enemies look ridiculous. Men found her enthralling. She kept her lovers as friends, and in her maturity was the confidante of countless others, who crept away from their wives and mistresses for an hour or two in her private sitting-room to enjoy the full flavour of her caustic humour and her worldly wisdom. She disliked scenes

31

as much as they did, had no use for sentimentality or the capriciousness of women and never asked awkward questions; and when Melbourne House became the centre of a scandal that rocked London in 1812, she was the only member of it who kept her head.

She disapproved from the beginning of the marriage of her favourite son William Lamb to Caroline, the daughter of Lady Bessborough. There was no love lost between the two mothers-in-law and Caroline was a wild, undisciplined young woman with a fiercely egocentric nature, totally unsuited to the young man who was eventually to become Queen Victoria's first Prime Minister. Lady Melbourne, however, gave the young couple a suite of apartments on the first floor at Melbourne House and for a time things did not go too badly, though cracks were beginning to appear in the conjugal harmony of their relationship some time before the author of *Childe Harold's Pilgrimage* woke up one morning in the spring of 1812 to find all London at his feet.

Byron's sensational poem with its romantic pessimism, its glowing rhetoric and colourful foreign background to the dissipation and sin of a picturesque young hero steeped in melancholy, set the town on fire. The poet himself, with his dishevelled curls, rapt expression and aloof manners seemed to be the very embodiment of his own hero. 'Bad, mad and dangerous to know' was Caroline Lamb's verdict when she first saw him. Not that she could have avoided knowing him even if she had wanted to. Such a lion—a poet and a peer, handsome, dissipated and exotic in his tastes—had not appeared in London society within living memory. All the drawing-rooms in Mayfair were thrown open to receive him; footmen crowded round his lodgings in St James's Street to deliver invitations from their high-born ladies and some of their lords as well, for no ball, assembly, rout or reception could be considered a success without the magnetic figure of Lord Byron. Everyone was talking about him, everyone wanted to meet him, or to be seen in his company. Even middle-class misses were begging or borrowing *Childe Harold* to read in the privacy of their own rooms with a swooning, love-sick sense of shame and a burning delight.

Meanwhile Caroline Lamb pursued him with an hysterical persistence in private and in public, and more than ever when his conquest of her began to bore him. Driven by a neurotic frenzy and the unsatisfied urge to show off, she could not leave him alone. Disguised as a page-boy in scarlet pantaloons, a silver-laced jacket and a plumed hat, she often appeared in his rooms unannounced and alone; and he was at a loss to know what to do with her, or with himself. The pose he adopted of a romantic lover did not really suit him; it covered an acute loneliness, a pathological fear of ridicule occasioned by his deformed foot, and a morbid sense of doom. So he was glad to get away from the passionate, feverish young woman upstairs to the sane and amusing woman downstairs, to leave Caroline rolling on the floor in a fit and to find Lady Melbourne calmly sitting on her sofa, mistress of herself and of the art of pleasing men and ever ready to entertain him with her wit and the wisdom of an older woman, who was not too old to find him attractive.

Lady Melbourne implied that it was all Caroline's fault and did not disapprove of Byron's growing desire to disentangle himself, though his methods were cruel and cynical. So long as they quarrelled in private there was nothing shocking in the affair and the gossip was rather amusing. But when Caroline, to revenge herself on Byron for his neglect of her, deliberately slashed her wrists with a broken glass at Lady Heathcote's ball in full view of the assembled company, her exhibitionism at last put her outside the pale of society. Byron looked on with a crooked smile, not altogether displeased at having provoked such a dreadful scene. Caroline was hurried off to the Melbournes' country house, Brocket Hall near Hertford, with her unfortunate husband William Lamb to take care of her, and Lady Melbourne wrote somewhat scornfully: 'I could not have believed it possible for any one to carry absurdity to such a pitch.'

No one paid very much attention to William Lamb's feelings in the uproar that ensued, though he was at the lowest ebb of his career and much in need of sympathy. His elder brother having died of consumption, he was now the heir to his father's peerage and had taken up a parliamentary career, which was not going at all well. In fact, he gave up his seat in the House of Commons in 1812 because he did not agree with the policy of the Whigs and at the same time felt he could not desert them for the Tories. However much his conscience leaned towards the moderate Tories led by Canning, his loyalty to the Whigs remained a moral conviction, emphasized by his birth and his heredity; and thus for the time being he stood in a no-man's-land, scarred by the infidelity of the impossible wife he still loved and by the uncertainty of his own political future. No. 10 Downing Street, the Prime Minister's official residence since Sir Robert Walpole had made it so in 1731, was only a step away from Melbourne House, but William Lamb was still a very long way from it.

Fig. 13 *House of Commons in 1808. By Rowlandson and Pugin*
(Hulton Picture Library)

Parliament met in the huddle of ancient Gothic buildings surrounding Westminster Hall, now all that is left of the great royal
Palace of Westminster begun by William Rufus at the end of the
eleventh century and remodelled by King Richard II. The chamber
of the House of Commons, originally the fourteenth-century chapel
of St Stephen, ran at right angles to the Hall, and although enlarged
and panelled by Wren in the reign of Queen Anne, was not much
more commodious for the Regency members of Parliament (*Fig. 13*)
than it had been for the members of King Edward VI's Parliament
meeting there for the first time in 1547. It was lit by candles in a
chandelier hanging above the Speaker's chair and the green baize
table bearing the Mace; and there was little or no ventilation, so that
the heat and the stuffiness when members crowded in for an important
debate, became intolerable. Their behaviour, according to most

34

observers, was totally lacking in dignity. They lolled on the benches with their hats tilted over their eyes, leaned against the pillars, stamped their feet, snuffled into their neckcloths, yawned, whispered, coughed and sometimes yelled like foxhounds at feeding time. The country members in their beaver hats and heavy boots were despised and laughed at by the more sophisticated Londoners; yet they sacrificed the rural pleasures they enjoyed to undertake their duties in the House, and it was by the courage and the common sense of these ordinary-looking men from the Shires that the Government was able to lead the country to victory over the tyranny of Napoleon.

Parliamentary eloquence had never reached greater heights than in the days of William Pitt, Fox and Sheridan; and when Pitt died in 1806, followed a few months later by Fox (*Fig. 14*), there were no orators of quite the same calibre, Sheridan having taken to the bottle and fallen into debt. Parliament, however, continued to wield the nation's power and purse and the royal prerogative was confined to

Fig. 14 *Charles James Fox, 1749–1806. By K. A. Hickel*
(National Portrait Gallery)

choosing the ministers of the Crown from the party with a majority in the House. The Whigs, after so many years in Opposition, had put their faith in the Prince of Wales. Fox and Sheridan had taught him all he knew about politics; the Devonshires, the Hollands, the Melbournes and the Grenvilles were his friends, and their hopes ran high every time the old King, George III, lapsed into madness. But the Prince, unlike William Lamb, had no compunction in throwing his friends over when at last he was designated Regent in 1811, and they never forgave him—or his new favourite, Lady Hertford, for whom he had forsaken Mrs Fitzherbert and Lady Jersey. Indeed it seemed that the infatuated Prince had become quite incapable of making any decision without the approval of this high and haughty Tory lady, already past her prime in looks and magnetism. Every afternoon his yellow chariot was to be seen driving through London with the purple blinds drawn, towards Hertford House in Manchester Square, and there, the Marquis stood to receive him, tactfully bowing himself backwards out of the drawing-room as soon as his royal guest had settled on a couch beside his connubial lady.

Yet the influence of Lady Hertford was not the only factor which turned the Regent against his former friends. In choosing Pitt's disciples to run the country, he was not such a fool as he seemed. The Whigs were hopelessly divided in their aims, whereas the Tories were intent on prosecuting the war with undiminished vigour. Without their support, Wellington's army in the Peninsula might have failed and without the diplomatic energy of Castlereagh and Vansittart in arranging loans to the oppressed Continental countries, Napoleon could never have been defeated. As it was, the ascending scale of victories won by Wellington at Talavera, Salamanca and Vittoria turned the tide, and early in 1814 Napoleon abdicated and retired to Elba, leaving the British and their allies the masters of Europe. All this should have made the Regent wildly popular with his people, but it did nothing of the kind. The Whigs, led by the wily Henry Brougham, stirred up the populace against him by championing the cause of his ugly and resentful wife, Princess Caroline, and their only daughter, Princess Charlotte; and by the time the Allied Sovereigns reached London in the summer of 1814 to celebrate the Peace, the Regent was thoroughly frightened of appearing in the streets and being hooted by the mob.

He was in a very unfortunate position. It should have been his crowning hour of glory and splendour as the head of the triumphant

British nation; he had waited long enough for this moment under the shadow of his father's insanity and of Napoleon's aggressive power in Europe. But by now, though only in his early fifties, self-indulgence and his appetite for pleasure, too much cherry brandy and too many chocolate éclairs had not improved his appearance or his temper. He was putting on weight. His 'brace-makers', Messrs Harboro & Acock of Cockspur Street, also 'stock and shirt-makers, glovers and hosiers' (now in Bond Street) had a job to satisfy him with the most intimate of all his garments and his valet had to lace him into them before he could don his skin-tight 'inexpressibles' and the well-cut coat of 'the First Gentleman in Europe'. And he was highly sensitive to ridicule, vain of his appearance, easily provoked, like a petulant, spoilt child, yet pitifully anxious to be loved and to create a good impression.

No expense was spared on the entertainment of his foreign guests. Carlton House had been redecorated and furnished with magnificent chandeliers and pier-glasses reflecting the forest of Ionic columns in the Circular Dining-Room; with velvet carpets adorned with the insignia of the Garter in the Crimson Drawing-Room, and with splendid ostrich plumes waving above the silver helmets of the high canopy in the Throne Room. The open double doors between the State Apartments on the ground floor gave a superb vista 350 feet long towards the Conservatory, a tented Gothic structure with clustered columns, a traceried ceiling encrusted with gold ornamentation and stained-glass windows opening on to the ravishing garden, where nightingales sang and the weeping willows swayed in the evening breeze. Yet the extravagant gala the Regent put on for the Allied Sovereigns was not a success. The Tsar of Russia, resplendent in a bottle-green velvet uniform laced with gold and dripping with diamond stars, merely bowed to Lady Hertford and refused to address a single word to her.

And it was all the more galling for the Regent that this blonde and handsome Muscovite with long legs and a waist as slender as a girl's should become the absolute idol of London. Aristocratic ladies in flimsy muslin dresses, with bare shoulders and jewels in their hair, fainted with joy at the sight of him and were sick with envy when he waltzed with Lady Jersey or the Countess Lieven at Almack's, the fashionable Assembly Rooms in King Street. All day and all night vast crowds stood outside Pulteney's Hotel in Piccadilly where he had elected to stay with his sister, the Grand Duchess Catherine of Oldenburg, instead of accepting the Regent's hospitality; and every time he appeared, his carriage was followed by a shouting, cheering mob, whose huzzas turned to hisses when their own royal master ventured out. The Regent was annoyed and upset. In the midst of all the pageantry and the processions, at the Lord Mayor's Banquet and the gala performance at Covent Garden, at the splendid review of his victorious armies in Hyde Park, he was constantly humiliated and forced to play second fiddle, and he did not like it at all. He was, according to Creevey, 'quite worn out with fuss, fatigue and rage' and thankful when the Tsar of Russia and the other royal princes left the shores of England.

The summer of rejoicing did not, however, end with their departure. The return of Wellington was the signal for a fresh outburst of excitement. Londoners would have taken the horses out of his carriage as it crossed Westminster Bridge to haul it through the streets in triumph, if he had not forestalled them by jumping on a horse and galloping off alone. The Government voted him £400,000 to buy an estate in the country and a town house at Hyde Park Corner, and the Regent presented him with a gold Field-Marshal's baton made by the London goldsmiths Rundell, Bridge & Rundell. His gallant officers received an equally enthusiastic welcome. Captain Gronow of the Foot Guards, arriving in St James's Street from Paris, wrote years later: 'I never shall forget the reception I met with as I dashed up in a chaise and four to the door of Fenton's Hotel. A mob of about a thousand people gathered round as I got out in my old weather-beaten uniform, shaking hands with me and uttering loud cheers.' But the rank and file fared less well. Brought home in leaky, over-crowded transports, the army was promptly disbanded to reduce taxation and at Chelsea, thousands of idle men hung around the doors of the public houses, drinking what they could get and fighting each other in desperation. 'There hobbled the maimed light infantryman, the heavy dragoon, the hussar and the artilleryman,' wrote Rifleman Harris, himself discharged after seven years' campaigning with a wound pension of 6d. a day; and he was luckier than most of his comrades, for the country had no use for its soldiers and its seamen now the war was over and their heroic deeds were done.

The Regent, meanwhile, was busy preparing the biggest spectacle he had ever conceived for London as the climax to the peace celebrations; but he took so long about it and changed his mind so often, the event could not be properly organized until the month of August, by which time rejoicings for the peace were becoming a little stale and it was decided to celebrate the centenary of the Hanoverian

Fig. 15 *Chinese Pagoda and Bridge designed by Nash. By J. P. Neale*
(Mansell Collection)

succession to the throne instead. The Royal Parks were thrown open
to the populace, with gambling and drinking booths in Hyde Park
and a mock naval battle on the Serpentine; a sham Castle of Discord
in Green Park, timed to explode at midnight to reveal a revolving
Temple of Peace, hopefully attended by a chorus of Vestal Virgins
in transparent draperies designed by the Prince himself; and a
seven-storeyed Chinese Pagoda (*Fig. 15*) on the bridge over the
canal in St James's Park, which did explode accidentally in the midst
of the firework display, killing one spectator, though everyone else
thought its column of fire was an intended part of the fun.

More than half a million people poured into the area to picnic on
the grass and gape at all the wonders displayed; and contrary to the
expectations of those who were hoping to make the Regent look
ridiculous, they were good-humoured and gay, and they enjoyed
themselves immensely. The Prince had personally selected the
Roman Candles, Girandoles, Jerbs and Gillocks in brilliant fire for
the final blaze of excitement, and Charles Lamb, standing in the
crowd, thought the rockets 'in clusters, in trees and all shapes, spread-

ing about like young stars in the making' were splendid. But the aftermath was not so pleasant. 'All that was countryfy'd in the Parks is all but obliterated,' he wrote. 'The very colour of the green is vanished, the whole surface of Hyde Park is dry crumbling sand (*Arabia Arenosa*), not a vestige or hint of green ever having grown there; booths and drinking places go all around it for a mile and a half . . . the stench in liquors, bad tobacco, dirty people and provisions conquers the air, and we are stifled and suffocated.' Indeed, the more raffish elements of the populace stayed in the gambling booths, drinking and whoring, long after the celebrations were over—and were still there a week later when Lord Sidmouth, the Home Secretary, had to intervene to extinguish their rowdy behaviour.

He did not succeed. The populace were a law unto themselves. It was not surprising if the Regent was nervous of them and kept out of their way. But in 1820 his old, mad father died at Windsor and he was Regent no longer. The heralds on the steps of the Mansion House and in the forecourt of St James's Palace proclaimed him King George IV, and he promptly became very ill when his virago of a wife not only threatened to return from her Continental travels to claim her rights as his Queen, but actually arrived in London a few weeks later and was acclaimed by the populace as a virtuous heroine who had been much abused by her husband and his Tory advisers. The Coronation was put off for twelve months and a Bill of Pains and Penalties brought against the Queen in the House of Lords, where the sordid details of her conduct were examined with such solemn and prolonged deliberation that even the mob, stirred up by the Whig Opposition, grew tired of sympathizing with her (*Fig. 16*). No one really believed in her innocence. Rouged and bewigged like a marmalade cat, hung with vulgar gobbets of jewellery and tatty velvet, she grossly overacted her part; and although the Bill was finally dropped, she had already become a bore and nuisance by the time Parliament had decided on the date of the Coronation and the King had made up his mind to face his people within and without the historic precincts of Westminster Abbey and Westminster Hall.

He was determined to make it a splendid occasion, though the Abbey itself was crumbling with neglect and it was so long—sixty years—since the last Coronation no one was quite certain what form of procedure should be followed at the ceremony. The King spent the night at the Speaker's House and kept everyone waiting half an hour in the morning, because one of the royal silk stockings was torn by the Great Chamberlain in the process of getting him

Fig. 16 *Lampoon on Queen Caroline. Published 1821* (Hulton Picture (Library)

dressed. None the less, when he finally entered Westminster Hall which was packed with peers and peeresses and court officials, his appearance was magnificent. Benjamin Haydon was an eye-witness of this great moment. 'Something rustles,' he wrote afterwards, 'and a being buried in satin, feathers and diamonds rolls gracefully into his seat. The room rises with a sort of feathered, silken thunder. Plumes wave, eyes sparkle, glasses are out, mouths smile and one

41

Fig. 17 *Royal Banquet after the Coronation of George IV, 1821. By Robert Havell* (National Portrait Gallery)

man becomes the prime object of attraction to thousands. The way in which the King bowed was really royal. As he looked towards the peeresses and the foreign ambassadors, he showed like some gorgeous bird of the East.' And as the huge procession formed up round the King and moved along the covered way from the Hall to the Abbey with the white-robed herbwomen strewing flowers and sweet-scented leaves along the royal path, the enormous crowds gave him a splendid reception. The famous pugilists lining the route had no need to use their strength, and even the counter-cheers for Queen Caroline were drowned. Forbidden to attend the ceremony, she had driven to the Abbey in her own carriage and finding the doors locked against her, had retired in confusion amid the boos and catcalls of the people, who had no intention of allowing her to spoil their enjoyment of the biggest and most costly royal pageant they had ever seen.

The ceremonies in the Abbey lasted until four o'clock in the afternoon and were followed by a gargantuan banquet in Westminster Hall (*Fig. 17*), where the King's Champion, heralded by 'a long and cheerful flourish of trumpets', appeared on horseback to throw down the challenge. Mounted on a piebald horse borrowed from Astley's Circus and attended by the Duke of Wellington as Lord High Constable and the deputy Earl Marshal, Lord Howard of Effingham, the Champion, clad in shining armour, flung down the gauntlet three times, was toasted by the King in a gold cup brimming with champagne and backed his horse manfully down the whole length of the Hall to loud applause. The feasting which followed this traditional demonstration and went on for more than four hours, was aggravated somewhat by the blobs of candle grease dripping from the twenty-eight magnificent lustres hanging from the hammer-beam roof; but more than eight tons of beef, veal and mutton were consumed, together with a huge number of geese and capons stuffed with apples, mushrooms and truffles, 280 dishes of fish, 160 tureens of soup, 480 boats of sauces and 1,000 dishes of pastry, jellies and creams. And this was only for the favoured guests at the tables spread on the floor of the great Hall. The spectators in the galleries erected round the walls were starving by the time the overfed and weary King left for Carlton House. Famished judges, privy councillors, knights of the Bath and the Thistle and their ladies fell upon the remains of the feast and later were to be seen asleep in the corridors or desperately wandering around the still crowded streets of Westminster in search of their carriages.

This was the last great Coronation Banquet ever to be held in Westminster Hall—and perhaps it was as well. The exhausted ladies and gentlemen of the Court forgot their manners and 'scenes were presented extremely at variance with the splendid spectacle which had been but a few hours before exhibited', while the mob outside was only prevented with the greatest difficulty from entering the Hall to plunder some of the 1,200 empty champagne bottles, the chicken bones and the silver spoons.

CHAPTER FOUR

The Regent and his Architect

'Once, and once only,' as Sir John Summerson says in his book *Georgian London*, 'has a great plan for London, affecting the capital as a whole, been projected and carried to completion'—and this was entirely due to the Prince Regent and his favourite architect, John Nash (*Fig. 18*).

How the association between them began remains something of a mystery. Nash was born in Lambeth of humble parents and worked for a time in Sir Robert Taylor's architectural office in the City, but his first venture on his own as a speculative builder in 1782 was a failure. He took the lease of three houses in Bloomsbury Square (now the premises of the Pharmaceutical Society of Great Britain), knocked them into one and covered the exterior with stucco—an unheard-of procedure at this time—placing a row of Corinthian pilasters on the façade to give the whole building an imposing appearance. Always optimistic and extremely ambitious in his ideas, he hoped to make his fortune from this project, but instead was declared a bankrupt and withdrew hastily to Wales where his widowed mother was living. In Carmarthen he made friends with some of the local gentry and was soon on such good terms with them, he obtained several commissions for remodelling and redesigning their country houses, besides finding work with the civic authority as the designer and builder of the new County Gaol.

Within a few years he had quite forgotten his earlier disaster and had built up a very promising connection in Wales, which he presently extended to Hereford and the West Country and developed still further by associating himself with Humphrey Repton, the most sought-after landscape gardener of the day. From Repton he learnt to look for the character of the landscape and to design his buildings

44

within the framework suggested by their natural surroundings—or, more exactly, by the ornamental surroundings so artfully contrived by Repton as to appear natural. Sometimes he used the picturesque Gothic style for his country houses, sometimes the classical Palladian villa form, but all his designs in whatever style he adopted were distinguished by his own vigorous personality. He had a buccaneering sort of temperament combined with an astonishing flair for thinking up adventurous ideas, and was always willing to risk his reputation for any of his schemes, even to back them with his own money if necessary in the belief that he would somehow come out on top; and indeed, as the years went on, though he was often in debt and suffered a great deal of criticism, his ebullient faith in himself was more than justified.

In 1798 he returned to London and apparently, when Repton was engaged by the Prince to landscape the garden of the Pavilion at Brighton, was brought in to design a new conservatory there. He evidently made a good impression on the Prince, and the young wife he married in the same year made a still better impression. Or it may have been that Mary Anne Nash, the attractive daughter of a coal merchant named Bradley, had already known the amorous Prince in his salad days, for between his more serious affairs with 'Perdita' Robinson, Mrs Fitzherbert and Lady Jersey, there had been quite a number of pretty middle-class maidens led up the back stairs at Carlton House for the pleasure of His Royal Highness. Whatever the truth, Mr and Mrs Nash suddenly blossomed out with a town house in Dover Street and a castellated residence at East Cowes in the Isle of Wight, and their close intimacy with the Prince was noticed by more than one observer. Not much official work seemed to come Nash's way at this time, but in 1806, when he was fifty-four, he accepted the obscure post of architect to the department of Woods and Forests and this was soon to launch him into the most brilliant phase of his whole career.

Marylebone Park, a wide area north of the New Road, originally the royal hunting park of King Henry VIII and now leased out as farmland, was due to revert to the Crown in 1811. It had already been the subject of four different reports made by John Fordyce, the Surveyor General to His Majesty's Land Revenues, for it was plain by the end of the eighteenth century that this large tract of virgin land could not remain undeveloped for very much longer and that if it could be developed successfully, it might yield a very substantial amount of revenue. Nothing, however, came of the competition

45

Fig. 18 *John Nash. Bust by W. Behnes,*
1831 (Hulton Picture Library)

suggested by the Surveyor General and as a last resort it was decided
to invite the architects of the Land Revenues department and of the
Woods and Forests to submit plans and proposals. Leverton and
Chawner of the Land Revenues produced a dull, unimaginative plan
extending the grid pattern of terraced houses that already covered
the Portman and Harley Estates northwards into the Park, while
reserving a small space for a few individually sited villas on the peri-
meter of St John's Wood. Nash, on the other hand, inspired by the
immense possibilities of this unique opportunity, sent in a report
that was revolutionary in its conception, masterly in its analysis of
what was required to transform the whole area into a new townscape
set within the leafy surroundings of a country park, and more
ambitious than anything which had yet been thought of for the general
improvement of London.

He began by stating the principles behind his plan in no uncertain
manner: 'That Mary-le-bone Park shall be made to contribute to the
healthfulness, beauty and advantage of that quarter of the Metropolis;
that the Houses and Buildings to be erected shall be of that useful
description and permanent construction, and shall possess such local

advantages as shall be likely to assure a great augmentation of Revenue to the Crown at the expiration of the Leases; that the attraction of open Space, free air and the scenery of Nature, with the means and invitation of exercise on horseback, on foot and in Carriages, shall be preserved or created in Mary-le-bone Park, as allurements or motives for the wealthy part of the Public to establish themselves there.' In fact, the Park was to be an exclusive, self-contained residential estate, where the urban architecture would be matched with an idyllic country landscape and nothing mean or ugly would be allowed to intrude. The needs of the wealthy part of the public who fell for these allurements, would be served by three markets lying outside the eastern edge of the Park, where a number of shops and smaller houses would be built for the essential tradesmen to inhabit, and by a branch of the new canal, which had been projected a year or two earlier.

For the central area of the Park, Nash proposed a great double circus with a 'National Valhalla' standing on rising ground in the middle of it; some forty or fifty private villas set in their own grounds in such a way that 'no Villa should see any other, but each should appear to possess the whole of the Park'; and a *guinguette* or Pleasure Pavilion for the Prince, overlooking a straight, formal stretch of water on the east side. Without acknowledging his debt to Humphrey Repton, since they had quarrelled some years earlier, he planned an artificial lake with three serpentine branches, very much in the Reptonian manner, as the main feature of his landscape. Earth from the excavation of the lake was to be piled up in undulating slopes to vary the level of the ground within the Inner Circle and the view to the north left open to the rural heights of Hampstead and Highgate. A drive, called the Outer Circle, ran all round the boundary, and here again the architect's proposals for a series of terraces faced with stucco and with the appearance of palatial country houses, took into account the picturesque effect of the whole. Another circus, with a church at the centre of it, was to cross the New Road at the north end of Portland Place to provide an elegant link between the older part of London and the new.

Something even more drastic, however, was called for if the new scheme was to attract the right kind of high class resident, especially those members of the House of Lords and the House of Commons who required direct access to Westminster. Portland Place, built by the Adam brothers and considered by Nash to be 'the finest street in London', was still a private enclosure. To get from Marylebone to Westminster it was necessary to travel down New and Old Bond

Street through all the density of the traffic, or along the narrow, tortuous streets of Soho, where poverty and neglect were only too obvious. The urgent need for better communication between the two areas was stressed by John Fordyce in his last report on Marylebone Park in 1809, but again nothing was done, though one or two suggestions were put forward for widening the Swallow Streets, north and south, and the Portland Road. Only Nash, with his marvellous breadth of vision, was capable of approaching the problem from a fresh angle and of providing a solution, which he presented with his usual energy and aplomb in his report on the Park.

He proposed to cut a new street altogether from the south end of Portland Place to the frontage of Carlton House in Pall Mall; 'to make a complete separation between the Streets and Squares occupied by the Nobility and Gentry, and the narrow Streets and meaner Houses occupied by mechanics and the trading part of the community'; and to give London a splendid processional way over a mile long. Taking the exceptional width of Portland Place as his yardstick, he drew a line of demarcation between Soho and the West End that turned slightly to the east where it crossed Oxford Street and farther south, curved gently towards Piccadilly to come into line with the straight section leading directly to Carlton House. Furthermore, he proposed a continuous colonnade to run the whole length of the street to enhance the grandeur and the dignity of its overall appearance. 'The beauty of the Town, it is presumed, would be advanced by a street of such magnificent dimensions,' he wrote, 'by the Colonnades and Balustrades which will adorn its sides . . . by the vista between Carlton House and Piccadilly terminated by a public monument at one end and by the Palace of Carlton House at the other'; while to add to the beauty of the approach from Westminster to Charing Cross, he suggested that 'a Square or Crescent, open to and looking down Parliament Street, might be built round the Equestrian Statue at Charing Cross'—thus introducing the theme of what was eventually to become Trafalgar Square.

The idea was as bold at it was comprehensive, and even the officials concerned in the negotiations realized its possibilities at once. As for the Regent, he was so pleased with Nash's magnificent plan, he was soon boasting that London would quite eclipse the splendours of Napoleon's Paris. But it was one thing for the plans to be approved by the Crown Commissioners, Parliament and the Treasury, and quite another thing for them to be carried out on the scale envisaged by Nash and the Prince. Both Regent's Park and Regent Street were speculative ventures. Public funds were available only for the gravel drives and the planting of the trees in the Park, and for compensation to the tradesmen and shopkeepers whose premises were demolished to make way for Regent Street. Building sites were leased to private builders, who were responsible for carrying out Nash's designs and hoped to make a profit from the quick sale of the houses and business premises as they were completed. But after the first wave of enthusiasm for the exciting new project began to recede, everything that could go wrong, did.

Mr Mayor, who started building the Circus at the north end of Portland Place (now Park Crescent) went bankrupt and one section of the houses collapsed altogether. The promised loan of £300,000 from the Globe Insurance Company for the making of Regent Street never materialized, and enquiries for the sites petered out, while Londoners watched the demolition in progress with a sardonic grin. Anyone less optimistic and without the superb self-confidence of Nash might have given up in despair and it was fortunate that he had the courage and the gambling spirit of an *entrepreneur* as well as the enthusiasm of a born artist of great ability. He was criticized by the Commissioners, by his professional colleagues, by the money-lenders and the builders—by everyone, except the Regent, so erratic and unpredictable in some ways, yet so constant and so faithful in support of his architect. Together they struggled against all the odds and in wartime, with prices fluctuating and the Commissioners waiting impatiently for the whole scheme to yield more than a handful of peppercorn rents; together they eventually achieved the one and only successful plan for the improvement of London ever to be accomplished in a single generation.

Regent Street progressed more quickly than the Park, gathering momentum after the battle of Waterloo when a boom in building set in, and being completed by 1823. It was a masterly achievement. With so many different developers working on the individual sites, Nash had to improvise to keep them happy without allowing them to destroy the unity of the street as a whole, and he succeeded brilliantly. The formal Ionic colonnades of the houses nearest to Carlton House set off the screen wall of the royal palace and were carried in a straight line to Piccadilly Circus, where instead of the public monument Nash had intended to close the vista, a full-sized replica of Inigo Jones's river façade to old Somerset House was built as the County Fire Office. From here the Quadrant (*Fig 19*) or quarter-circle began, designed and built by Nash himself as a strategic solution

49

Fig. 19 *The Quadrant, Regent Street. By T. H. Shepherd, 1827*
(Mansell Collection)

to the problem of changing the axis of the street. With its superb
colonnades consisting of one hundred and forty-five large columns
'worthy of a Roman amphitheatre', it was the most spectacular
section of the whole street and the most daring innovation. No one but
Nash would have been rash enough to undertake it or sufficiently
confident to have advanced more than £60,000 of his own money
to the bricklayers, plumbers, glaziers and other tradesmen he employed to get the work done. That he lost money over it in the end did
not seem to worry him very much; the achievement mattered more
than the cash.

Farther along the street, he permitted a greater diversity of buildings,
which none the less coalesced and fitted in with each other, being set
in proportion to the width and the scale of the street and all being
faced with the same gleaming, cream-coloured stucco that served to
give a brilliant finish to each individual block. The corners of the
side streets leading into Mayfair were terminated with circular,
domed buildings or elegant square-cut pavilions with 'shell' windows
on the first floor, opening on to balustraded balconies. Some of

50

these architectural details were better than others depending on the standards of the different builders and on how much time Nash himself was able to give to each structure, though his real genius was always expressed more fully in the wide sweep of his ideas than in paying any very meticulous attention to detail. At the crossing of Oxford Street, he designed another Circus to act as a pivot, and at the far end where the street swung round Foley House (afterwards Langham House) into Portland Place, he produced one of his most ingenious ideas by placing the circular portico and spire of All Souls church to mask what would otherwise have been the most awkward angle in his entire composition.

All Souls (restored after the Second World War) has survived, but as a focal point on the skyline has been totally destroyed by the latest extension to Broadcasting House, rising in a great cliff directly behind it. Regent Street itself suffered the loss of its colonnades as early as 1848 at the instigation of a certain Mr Crane, a hosier and glover and inventor of the 'Patent Belt Drawers', who complained that his shop was darkened by the arcading outside; and by 1927 all Nash's work, except the actual line of the street, had been swept away, this particular piece of twentieth century vandalism being celebrated by cheering spectators when King George V and Queen Mary drove down the heavily rebuilt street in a state landau amid flags and floral decorations.

Regent's Park has been luckier. Thanks to the recommendations of the Gorrell Committee in 1947 and to the vociferous public agitation led by John Betjeman in 1957, demolition was avoided and the Crown Commissioners were persuaded to restore the Nash Terraces or to rebuild them in replica where the structure was found to be faulty; and here, though the original plans were modified by Nash and some of his ideas had to be abandoned, it is still possible to enjoy his most glorious architectural panorama set within its own Elysian surroundings of mature trees, green lawns and the serpentine lake. Regent's Park, unique in the history of town planning and the ideal *rus in urbe*, has no equivalent anywhere in the world.

At the beginning, however, when Nash and the Regent were fighting for their new street, the Park hung fire. The failure of Mr Mayor, though retrieved by Nash himself by the building of Park Crescent instead of the circus he had originally planned, put off all other interested parties for the time being; and in 1816 the Commissioners were complaining that they had spent £53,650 4s. 2d. on planting and landscaping the area, or five times the amount estimated by Nash, without seeing any return. Only one villa, St John's Lodge (now used by Bedford College), had been built a year later and none of the proposed terraces. If it had not been for James Burton, one of the first men in the building trade to organize his craftsmen on a permanent basis instead of employing them piece-meal for each job, the whole plan might have come to nothing.

Burton had made a great deal of money in developing the Bedford Estate in Bloomsbury and now having plunged deeply into the scheme for Regent Street, he was astute enough to realize that if the Park failed to materialize as the main objective of the street, he would lose heavily on his investment; so he took up one of the villa sites on the edge of the lake in 1818 and built himself a house there, called The Holme (now used by Bedford College). It was designed by his eighteen-year-old son Decimus and marked the beginning of this young man's highly successful career as an architect working in close collaboration with Nash. Three years later he designed and built Cornwall Terrace with its fine end house, characterized by the large bay window decorated with four charming caryatids; and then went on, with Nash's approval, to undertake Clarence Terrace and Grove House, one of the most imposing villas on the north-west boundary of the Park (now belonging to the Nuffield Foundation). Hertford Villa, built for the 3rd Marquis of Hertford, and Holford House were also designed by Decimus Burton, but the former, after serving as the headquarters of St Dunstan's, was rebuilt in a neo-Georgian style for Barbara Hutton in 1939 and later handed over to the American Embassy, while the latter was totally destroyed by enemy action during the war.

Meanwhile, James Burton and Nash co-operated in other areas of the Park. Though their relations were not always very cordial, they could not really do without each other, Burton putting up the money and undertaking the construction of York Terrace and Nash changing his design at York Gate to frame the vista of the new church designed by Thomas Hardwick for the St Marylebone vestry, who had re-linquished their original site at the end of Portland Place. This gave a second entrance to the Park from the New Road, as elegant and as effective as Park Crescent; and from this time on, the whole scheme began to move forward at a pace. Park Square, Sussex Place with its ten domes and fifty-six Corinthian columns, Kent Terrace and Han-over Terrace were all built by 1823; and finally, between 1826 and 1828, one minor terrace, Gloucester Gate, and the last two major ones, Cumberland and Chester, were completed.

Fig. 20 *Cumberland Terrace today* (Photo: A. F. Kersting)

Cumberland Terrace (*Fig. 20*) with its seven porticoes, its pediments and arches, was—and still is—as Nash intended it to be, the most splendid of all his architectural designs and perhaps the most exciting; but Chester, with its graceful Ionic columns and triumphal arches, forms an equally marvellous composition, and Nash had good reason to be proud of himself. He had been forced to abandon his 'National Valhalla', some of the villas and the circus in the Inner Circle, and the *guinguette* for his royal master who had made a pleasure dome of the Pavilion at Brighton instead. But, now in his seventies and by his own account 'a thick, squat, dwarf figure with a round head, snub nose and little eyes', he had achieved what he had set out to do and had created the most civilized and the most lyrical environment ever imagined as a residential quarter within walking distance of central London (*Fig. 21*). It remained only for his pupil, Decimus Burton, to design the immense Colosseum in 1829, where a grand

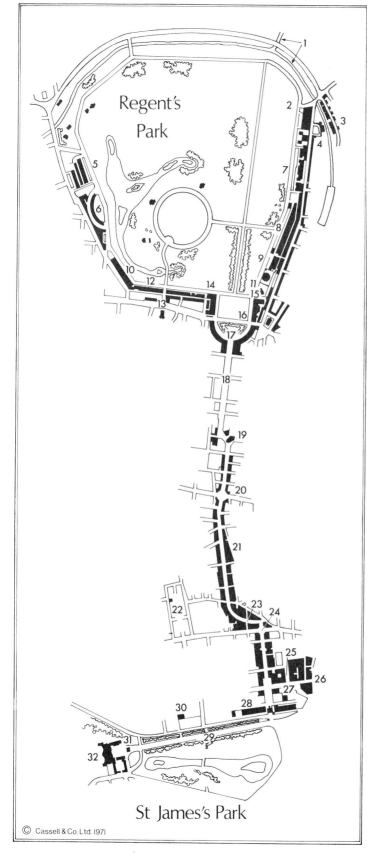

Fig. 21 *Map of the developments executed by Nash from Regent's Park to St James's Park.*

1. Regent's Canal
2. Gloucester Gate
3. Park Village East
4. Park Village West
5. Hanover Terrace
6. Sussex Place
7. Cumberland Terrace
8. Chester Terrace
9. Cambridge Terrace
10. Cornwall Terrace
11. Someries House
12. York Terrace
13. York Gate
14. Ulster Terrace
15. St Andrew's Place
16. Park Square East
17. Park Crescent
18. Portland Place
19. All Souls, Langham Place
20. Oxford Circus
21. Regent Street
22. Dover Street
23. The Quadrant
24. Piccadilly Circus
25. Suffolk Place
26. Suffolk Street
27. United Service Club
28. Carlton House Terrace
29. The Mall
30. Clarence House
31. The Marble Arch
32. Buckingham Palace

panorama of London was put on view, and for his adopted son, James Pennethorne, to finish the two charming Park Villages, East and West, as a colony of picturesque cottages on the north-eastern fringe of the Park. Park Village West, off Albany Street, is still intact and Tower House in its leafy garden, a rural gem.

Contemporary opinion on the merits of Regent Street and the Park varied. James Elmes in his *Metropolitan Improvements*, published in 1827, compared the building achievements of the Regency with those of Athens under Pericles, Rome under Augustus and Paris under Louis XIV. He wrote a detailed and scholarly account of the developments 'which have metamorphosised Mary-le-bone Park farm and its cow-sheds into a rural city of almost eastern magnificence; and changed Swallow Street and its filthy labyrinthine environs into the most picturesque and splendid street in the metropolis'. While criticizing some of the meritricious and slipshod detail of the individual terraces in the Park, he was, none the less, at his most enthusiastic in describing how 'all the elegancies of the town and the beauties of the country are co-mingled with happy art and blissful union', and he recommended that 'in performing a tour of the Regent's Park on a fine day, the enquirer into its beauties and merits should perform it leisurely and on foot'—advice which is still worth following.

Prince Pückler-Muskau, who often visited Nash in the palatial new residence he had built for himself in Lower Regent Street, decorated with copies of Raphael's frescoes from the Vatican and models of the Apollo Belvedere and the Medici Venus, held much the same opinion as James Elmes. He thought the landscape gardening in the Park was faultless, especially in the disposition of the water, where 'art completely solved the difficult problem of concealing her operations under an appearance of unrestrained nature'. But he laughed at the sculpture on the pediment of Cumberland Terrace and 'among many such monstrosities', noticed particularly 'four figures squeezed flat against the wall . . . clad in a sort of dressing-gown', whose 'purpose or import' he found 'extremely mysterious' and quite inexplicable.

Maria Edgeworth, the novelist, on a visit to London in 1830, was also highly critical of Mr Bubb's not very good sculpture. Though 'properly surprised by the new town that has been built in the Regent's Park', she was indignant at 'plaister (sic) statues and horrid useless *domes* and pediments crowded with mock sculpture figures, which damp and smoke must destroy in a season or two,' adding, 'there is ever some voice which cries Must fall! Must fall! Must scale off—soon, soon, soon!' Crabb Robinson, however, writing with more perception, declared: 'I really think this enclosure, with the New Street leading to it from Carlton House, will give a sort of glory to the Regent's government, which will be more felt by posterity than the victories of Trafalgar and Waterloo, glorious as these are.'

Any other architect with so much work so successfully achieved might have been content to rest on his laurels in the hope of enjoying a more peaceful old age, free from the vexations he had suffered. But Nash was never given a chance to retire. Almost as soon as his 'Royal Mile' from Carlton House to the Park was finished, the Regent, now George IV, changed his mind again. He declared that Carlton House was virtually a slum, though he had spent millions on it; that it was shabby, inconvenient and unsafe. He had, in fact, as was his habit in casting off Mrs Fitzherbert for Lady Hertford and Lady Hertford for his last *inamorata*, Lady Conyngham, set his heart on a new adventure. He wanted to convert old Buckingham House on the far side of St James's Park into a palace fit for the British monarchy.

He said he objected to living in a street, in spite of the colonnade that screened Carlton House from the public eye and in spite of the magnificent view Nash had given him towards Piccadilly Circus and the other distinctive improvements he had made in the region of Pall Mall. The most important of these consisted of his brilliant reconstruction in 1816 of the King's Theatre (also called the Royal Italian Opera House) on the corner of Pall Mall and the Haymarket. Retaining the auditorium built in 1789 by a Polish architect, Novosielsky, on the site of Sir John Vanbrugh's still earlier theatre, he provided a grand front on the Haymarket with an arcade, which continued round the sides of the block into Pall Mall and King Charles Street and again round the western boundary of the site in a long, vaulted passage with small shops, known as the Royal Opera Arcade (now cleverly restored and incorporated into the modern block of New Zealand House). The whole design gave elegance to the Haymarket–Pall Mall corner and was further enhanced by the rebuilding of the Haymarket Theatre on a new site directly in line with King Charles Street, from where its columned portico can still be seen, and by the construction of Suffolk Street and Suffolk Place, one of the few surviving examples of Nash's street elevations.

Nothing, however, could deflect the King from his purpose once he had made up his mind that he wanted Buckingham House. The fact that he had spent a fortune on the Pavilion at Brighton and was now, in 1823, spending £150,000 on the reconditioning of Windsor Castle, did not deter him in the least. Two years later a Bill was passed in Parliament enabling the revenues of the Crown Lands to be applied to the remodelling of Buckingham House, and Nash's first estimate for 'essential repair and improvement' amounting to 'not less than £200,000' was approved—much to the delight of the King and greatly to the mortification of Soane, who was officially in charge of the royal palaces and thought the project should have been assigned to him. In the event, he dodged a great deal of trouble; for the enormous task was too much for the King, whose flamboyant dreams were becoming ever more extravagant as he grew older, and for his ageing architect, caught between the bizarre fantasies of his master and the mounting opposition of Parliament and the Treasury.

The plans sketched in rather a hurry by Nash and drawn by his assistant, A. C. Pugin, looked well enough on paper and the building in Bath stone was begun in good faith round the shell of the old house. But before long the lack of cohesion between the central portion and the side pavilions of the front elevation became apparent, and by 1827 the original estimate of £200,000 had already been grossly exceeded. The Treasury began to demur and Nash's enemies to gang up against him. His dome was called 'that common slop-pail turned upside down' and he was accused of every kind of trickery and incompetence. Public criticism was nothing new—he had triumphed over it before; public finance was a different matter and could not be so easily wangled. Yet once again his fertile imagination devised a solution of a sort—nothing less than the complete demolition of Carlton House and the development of the site as a source of revenue.

The two massive blocks he designed for Carlton House Terrace (*Fig. 22*) (still a glorious feature of St James's Park) were immediately successful and became the most expensive and the most fashionable address in London. They were conceived on a monumental scale with rows of giant Corinthian columns running the whole length of the façade, and a balustraded terrace supported by the superb sweep of Doric columns projecting on the lower ground level all along the Mall. Between them Nash intended to place a fountain covered by a circular temple, but this idea was never carried out and instead, the top of the steps leading from St James's Park into Waterloo Place became the site of Benjamin Wyatt's granite column erected in 1831 to the memory of the Duke of York. For the east side of Waterloo Place where it runs into Pall Mall, Nash designed new premises for the United Service Club and on the west, Decimus Burton erected the

Fig. 22 *Carlton House Terrace* (Photo: A. F. Kersting)

Athenaeum—to complete the formal layout with dignity and restraint. Later, in 1829, the very young architect Charles Barry, whose neo-Gothic design for the new Palace of Westminster was to make him famous in the future, added lustre to the development of Pall Mall with his adventurous, Italianate design for the Travellers' Club.

Nash, meanwhile, with Carlton House Terrace and Waterloo Place still under construction, was also occupied with Clarence House (now the home of Queen Elizabeth the Queen Mother) and with a proposal to build another range of terraces on the south side of St James's Park to offset Buckingham Palace—a plan which had to be abandoned for lack of funds, the site being used eventually for the Wellington Barracks, erected in 1834. He did, however, get permission from the Treasury to improve the Park, which at that time had a straight canal running down the middle of it and was, according to Prince Pückler-Muskau, 'only a sort of meadow for cows'. Here again, as in Regent's Park, by redesigning the whole area on picturesque lines, breaking the canal into a long, curly lake split round an island and planting the lawns with trees and flowering shrubs at different levels, he showed his genius for creating a landscape of the most ravishing beauty in the centre of the urban metropolis. Old and harassed by his many commitments, he still knew how to obtain the maximum effect in the minimum of space, directing the layout of each lyrical vista with an eye that never faltered.

But if his work in St James's Park was an unqualified success and a pleasure for the elderly architect, his engagement at Buckingham Palace (*Fig. 23*) was the exact opposite. Things there were going from bad to worse. The revenue from the Carlton House Terrace scheme was not enough, and in 1828 when the Duke of Wellington became Prime Minister, he tightened the purse strings, meeting the fury of the King and the dismay of the architect with a bland refusal to supply the extra cash needed to finish the job in the grand style conceived by His Majesty. Ravaccione marble had already been obtained by one of Nash's agents, named Browne, for the huge Roman arch to stand in front of the Palace as a triumphal gateway, and

Fig. 23 *Buckingham Palace from St James's Park. By Thomas Higham, circa 1830* (Hulton Picture Library)

Westmacott, Baily and Chantrey set to work on the sculpture. But this, too, was a white elephant; the state coach was too broad to pass comfortably through the centre arch. Poor James Browne had to pay the expenses of his journey to Italy out of his own pocket, and twenty years later, the Marble Arch was moved to its present site north of Hyde Park.

Marble for the Grand Hall and the Grand Staircase was likewise brought from Italy at tremendous cost and craftsmen set to work on the gilded bronze balustrading, which is still one of the finest examples of Regency metalwork. Some of the fixtures and fittings from Carlton House—the mantelpieces, the ornate mirrors and lustres—were installed in the State Apartments. But the seemingly endless work on the Palace was still unfinished by 1830, when the King died; and soon afterwards Nash was ignominiously dismissed in favour of Edward Blore, who proceeded to mask most of the building with a new front, which in turn gave place to Sir Aston Webb's elevation erected in 1913. Only the garden front remains to some extent as Nash originally conceived it.

His failure to achieve what was to have been the greatest of all his 'Metropolitan Improvements' was disastrous. Henceforth none of his contemporaries had a good word for Nash and his extravagant royal patron could protect him no longer from the public outcry that preceded his dismissal. It would, however, be totally wrong to judge the King or his favourite architect by the long drawn out and sad story of their mistakes at Buckingham Palace. For George IV, from the time he became Prince Regent until the day of his death, knew what he wanted for London and his taste in the visual arts, his passion for architecture and his initiative when matched with the vision of Nash as the bold interpreter of his dreams, gave the capital a new splendour, which is still to be found wherever their influence survives. The King may have been irresponsible and eccentric, with a florid taste in women and a greedy appetite for pleasure, and the architect a buccaneer with a dubious reputation for the financial side of the business, but the two of them together worked a miracle that has never been equalled or surpassed in the long history of London.

CHAPTER FIVE

High Society

One of the original objections to the plan for Regent Street came from the vestrymen of the parish of St James's, who complained that their shopkeepers would be ruined if trade were drawn away from them into the new street. In fact, their apprehension was groundless. St James's Street, Piccadilly, Bond Street and their surroundings remained the most exclusive shopping district in London, while the patronage of the Prince and of Beau Brummell, the absolute *arbiter elegantarium* of fashionable society, ensured the success of the select tradesmen who catered for their needs.

Brummell had arrived at his pre-eminence as the first of the dandies by way of Eton and a cornetcy in the Prince's own regiment, the 10th Hussars, resigning his commission when the Hussars were ordered to Manchester to suppress a riot in the cotton mills because he could not tolerate the idea of being exiled to a provincial town. Not in the least high-born—his grandfather was a valet and his father a self-made land agent—he set out to cultivate a personality and a manner superior to everyone else; and by a combination of outrageous impertinence, sarcasm and extreme arrogance, he succeeded. 'His maxims on dress were excellent,' according to Harriette Wilson, the queen of the demi-reps. 'He possessed also, a sort of quaint dry humour, not amounting to anything like wit; but his affected manners and little absurdities amused for the moment. Then it became the fashion to court Brummell's society, which was enough to make many seek it, who cared not for it; and many more wished to be well with him through fear, for all knew him to be cold, heartless and satirical.'

This was true. He took a malicious delight in snubbing his well-bred friends, as when the Duke of Bedford once asked his opinion of the coat he was wearing and Brummell, after looking him up and down, remarked: 'My dear fellow—did I hear you call that *thing* a coat?' And when he became altogether too cocksure of his own importance, he made rude remarks in a loud voice about the Prince's figure, which gave the sensitive Prince much pain and finally caused a rift between them. No one was permitted to question his authority. As the creator of a new style in dress of the utmost and most expensive simplicity, he believed that he alone knew what sartorial perfection was. He made the reputation of Weston, his tailor in Old Bond Street, and boasted of having his boots polished in the froth of champagne, while the fit of his gloves was ensured by employing one firm to cut the fingers and another the thumbs.

Tailors, hatters, glovers and shirtmakers were prepared to give Brummell extensive credit in return for his custom; and so self-absorbed was he in his appearance, he spent some five hours every morning at his toilet, first bathing in eau-de-Cologne and water, then giving an hour to his hairdresser and another two hours to 'creasing down' his starched cravat until he was satisfied with its immaculate folds (*Fig. 24*). A friend calling on him one morning at his house in Chesterfield Street, met his valet coming out of his dressing-room with a dozen or more pieces of crumpled muslin over his arm, which he described as 'our failures'; and when at last the Beau emerged at three o'clock in the afternoon in his skin-tight 'trowsers' and flawless coat, it was the impeccable balance of his snow-white 'starcher' that gave him an air of supreme self-confidence. As he strolled disdainfully across Piccadilly towards St James's Street, he took no notice of anyone, while aware that everyone was taking notice of him; and when he arrived at White's, it was only the members of the Club's select inner circle—the Duke of Argyll, Lords Alvanley, Sefton, Worcester and Foley, 'Poodle' Byng, 'Ball' Hughes and Sir Lumley Skeffington (*Fig. 25*)—who dared to join him in the bow-window, where he reigned supreme and his pronouncements were listened to as if he had the wisdom of Solomon, until some time later when his debts caught up with him and he was forced to make a quick escape across the Channel, to die at last in poverty and squalor in a lodging-house at Caen.

Captain Gronow in later years considered the fashionable dress of the Regency quite absurd; 'the stiff white cravat worn by the dandies,' he declared, 'prevented them from seeing their own boots while standing up.' But the shopkeepers in the area of St James's Street had every reason to be pleased with the extravagant

Fig. 24 *Beau Brummell. Engraved by J. Cooke*
from a miniature (Hulton Picture Library)

attention these gentlemen gave to their appearance. Their trade increased immeasurably and some of them made a fortune. Hoby, the most famous of all the bootmakers, on the corner of Piccadilly and St James's Street, died worth £120,000. He is said to have employed over three hundred workmen and to have had such a high opinion of himself as a bootmaker that he could afford to adopt 'rather an insolent tone' with some of his customers. He made military long boots, fashionable Hessian boots with a tassel dangling from the V-shaped front, Hussar boots to be worn with pantaloons, top boots worn with buckskins or breeches, Wellington boots and 'highlows', or ankle boots, worn with trousers; and he drove about London in style in a smart black tilbury drawn by a frisky black horse. In his spare time he took to preaching at a Methodist church in Islington, and when he heard of Wellington's victory over the French at Vittoria, he was reported to have said: 'If Lord Wellington had had any other bootmaker than myself, he never would have had his great and constant successes; for my boots and my prayers bring His Lordship out of all his difficulties.'

Hoby's premises were demolished in the nineteenth-century redevelopment of Piccadilly, but two of the original shops at the other end of St James's Street have survived into the twentieth century: Lock's the hatters at No. 6 and Berry Brothers, the world-famous wine merchants, at No. 3. Lock's had moved into No. 6 from the west side of the street as early as 1764 and was a family business. All their hats were made to measure and of the finest quality, from the beaver hats worn by the nobility and the gentry in the country to the glossy black top hats worn by the dandies in town and the *chapeau bras* which a gentleman carried folded up under his arm in the evening. Lord Nelson paid £2 6s. for the last cocked hat Lock's made for him with a green eye-shade attached to it to cover his blind eye, before he went aboard the *Victory* and sailed to Trafalgar. Officers of the Hussars and the Dragoons had to pay more for their beplumed and gold-laced shakos; but the pernickety dandies, whose custom was the best kind of advertisement, often managed to get away without paying any of their bills from one year to the next. Lord Alvanley, quite the wittiest of them all, said of a rich friend who had become poor, that 'he had muddled away his

Fig. 25 *Bond Street Loungers, 1820. Dukes of Devonshire and Beaufort, Lords Sefton and Manners, and Mr 'Poodle' Byng. By R. Dighton* (Mansell Collection)

fortune in paying tradesmen's bills'; and when his own financial affairs had reached a crisis, he wrote cheerfully to another friend from his house in Park Place off St James's Street; 'I have no credit with either butcher or poulterer, but if you can put up with turtle or turbot, I shall be delighted to see you here for dinner.'

Berry Brothers, the other surviving shop in St James's Street, was still a grocer's, which had been founded by a certain Widow Bourne at the sign of the Coffee Mill as early as 1699 and through intermarriage with the Pickering and Clarke families, had descended to George Berry in 1810. It was famous for its choice tea and coffee, its tobacco from the New World and spices from the Far East; and during the eighteenth century the practice had begun of weighing some of the customers who came into the shop on the great scales that the Widow Bourne had used for her huge bags of coffee. Brummell constantly tested his weight on the scales there, 'in boots' and 'out of boots', and sometimes 'in shoes and a frock'. The Prince Regent sat on the weighing machine when his figure was still reasonably good and Lord Petersham, famous for his Cossack trousers and the double-breasted coat named after him, was another somewhat eccentric client. He lived at Harrington House in Stable Yard round the corner from St James's Palace, and the shelves along the walls of his sitting-room were loaded with beautiful jars and canisters of Congue, Pekoe, Souchong, Bohea and many other varieties of tea, all of the best kind supplied by George Berry; and besides being a connoisseur of tea, he was an expert in the art of moistening, mixing and blending snuff. When he died, his 'snuff-cellar' was valued at £3,000 and it was discovered that he owned three hundred and sixty-five snuff boxes, one for every day of the year.

Expense was of no account to the dandies. It was considered bad form to question the cost of anything and none of them ever thought of living within their means or of practising the middle-class virtue of economy. Lord Alvanley for years insisted on having a fresh apricot tart on his side-table every day of the week in case he fancied a slice for his dinner, and he once organized a freak dinner at White's, which cost £108 5s. for one dish. On another occasion he ordered a hamper for eight people from Gunther's, the pastrycook's in Berkeley Square, which cost him £200. Gunther could charge what he liked; he was the most celebrated of all the confectioners in London, attributing his fame 'to a quick eye, a delicate tongue (both for tasting and speaking) and an extreme patience'. As well as 'all sorts of Biskets and Cakes, Fine and Common Sugar Plums', he made a speciality of 'all Sorts of Ices' and from time to time inserted a discreet advertisement in *The Times* announcing that 'Messrs Gunther respectfully beg to inform the Nobility and those who honour them with their commands, that having this day received one of their cargoes of ice by the *Platoff* from the Greenland Seas, they are enabled to supply their CREAM and FRUIT Ices at their former prices'. Before the cargo began to melt, the blocks of ice were buried in the ground under the cellars of Berkeley Square.

Gunther's remained in their original premises until the 1930s, when the east side of Berkeley Square was demolished and rebuilt with modern offices. Many of the exclusive shops in St James's Street, Piccadilly and Bond Street suffered a similar fate in the modernization of these streets; or, as with Hatchards bookshop in Piccadilly and with Fortnum & Mason, the business founded by George III's ex-footman Charles Fortnum, who joined up with another grocer called John Mason in 1817, have been rebuilt on their original sites. These shops have not lost their elegance on a larger scale; but the smaller shops in the Royal Opera Arcade off Pall Mall and the Burlington Arcade (*Fig. 26*) in Piccadilly, designed by Samuel Ware and opened in 1819, have retained still more of the atmosphere of the days when the Regency dandies had nothing to do except squander their money.

Fig. 26 *Burlington Arcade, Piccadilly. By T. H. Shepherd, 1828*
(Hulton Picture Library)

Society was dominated by their entirely selfish pursuit of leisure and pleasure. At the Clubs in St James's Street—White's, Boodle's and Brooks's, which have all survived—gambling was the members' main occupation. Hour after hour, with their hats tilted over their eyes, they stooped over the green baize tables, until fuddled with exhaustion and doomed by their appalling losses, they crept away in the early morning, round to the house of 'Jew' King in Clarges Street to mortgage their estates, or to Hamlet, the jeweller in Cranbourn Alley, to pledge their inherited gold and silver plate or their wives' diamonds for the loan of some extra cash. Whist, faro and hazard were an irresistible temptation and a curious kind of self-discipline also, since it was considered ill-bred for anyone to show his feelings when losing heavily, or to rejoice too heartily if fortune turned in his favour. Raggett, the proprietor of White's, used to sit up all through the night in the card room, sending his servants to bed, so that he could sweep the carpets himself in the early hours of the morning to retrieve the gold carelessly scattered on the floor.

Crockford, an ex-fishmonger, was even more successful. 'Seated snug and sly in the corner of the room, watchful as the dragon that guarded the golden apples of Hesperides', he made over £1,000,000 out of the gambling mania of the aristocracy and retired eventually to a mansion in Carlton House Terrace. His premises in St James's Street, designed by Benjamin Dean Wyatt in 1827, were the most palatial in London and very richly decorated. Suppers of the most exquisite kinds, prepared by his famous chef, Ude, were provided free of charge with the best wines and every luxury in season; and the members of the Club, according to Captain Gronow, included all the celebrities of England from the Duke of Wellington and the heroes of the Peninsular War down to the youngest Ensign in the Guards. 'Statesmen, poets and men of pleasure when "the House was up" and balls and parties at an end, delighted to finish the evening with a little supper and a good deal of Hazard at old Crockey's gay and festive board, which was constantly replenished from midnight to early dawn.' Lights shone from the windows of Benjamin Wyatt's *piano nobile* between the Corinthian pilasters, while Lord Alvanley, 'Ball' Hughes, 'King' Allen and later, Count d'Orsay, the young Disraeli and Bulwer Lytton hung upon the game of chance.

This was a man's world; the clubs, the shops and the smart hotels which began to prosper in the Regency, were all dedicated to serving the fashion-conscious dandies and the wealthy aristocracy. No lady who valued her reputation was to be seen walking down Bond Street or St James's Street in the afternoon; and in the morning she would have to be accompanied by her maid, a footman or a page to protect her from the lascivious glances of any gentlemen up early enough to find her attractive. The linen-drapers, silk mercers, haberdashers, dressmakers, milliners and corsetiers responsible for her wardrobe, were still situated around Leicester Square and Covent Garden, though some of them had moved to Oxford Street and Mayfair, and others, like Mr Swan and Mr Edgar, who came together in 1812, took premises in the new Regent Street. Clark & Debenham of Cavendish House, Wigmore Street (the future Debenham & Free-body) were well established by 1813, when they advertised 'A Large Assortment of Cottage Twills, Stuffs, Bombazines, Sarsnets, Satins, Millinery, Pelisses and Dresses'; and W. H. Botibol of Oxford Street, a *plumassier* by trade, offered his customers 'Ostrich and Fancy Feathers and Artificial Flowers' to adorn the huge gypsy hats and bonnets, which contrasted very fetchingly with the transparent muslin gowns so fashionable in the Regency. Anything termed *Parisienne*, even during the Napoleonic Wars, carried snobbish over-tones and a prestige stimulated by the fashionable monthly journals for women, *La Belle Assemblée* and *The Lady's Magazine*, whose editorial comments covered 'High Life and Fashionable Chit Chat, Continental Notes and *On-dits*'.

High life for the ladies was restricted to the balls and routs in private houses or to Almack's Assembly Rooms in King Street off St James's Street. Here a committee of seven high-born ladies ruled with absolute authority, since they alone had the privilege of granting vouchers of admission to the subscription balls on Wednesday evenings and no one was allowed in without their approval. The intrigue that went on to obtain the *entrée* to this exclusive temple of the *ton* occupied the time and energy of everyone; yet the pleasure of Almack's consisted almost entirely in being seen there and in standing about and quizzing the company, or in being able to refer casually the next morning to having spent the evening there. The refreshment, composed of lemonade and tea, bread and butter and stale cake, was unexciting, and the dancing very decorous and dull, until the wife of the Russian Ambassador, Countess Lieven, caused a sensation by introducing the waltz and whirling round the floor with 'Cupid' Palmerston. Lady Jersey, not to be outdone, took up the fashion and before long 'the seductive Waltz, the voluptuous Waltz', mocked at by Byron in his poem, *The Waltz*, was all the rage. Ladies and gentlemen practised at home in the mornings 'with unparalleled assiduity' and those who believed it was a shocking excuse for 'squeezing and hugging' were soon outnumbered.

Countess Lieven, a most alluring young woman with an infinite capacity for making mischief, quickly became one of London's leading hostesses. 'It is not fashionable where I am not,' she wrote to her brother, Count Benckendorff, in 1816. 'I amuse myself like the rest, I keep late hours and I dance . . . and without vanity I may say that my soirées and those of Lady Jersey are the most agreeable and the most brilliant.' First in Harley Street and then in the more luxurious Ashburnham House in Dover Street where the Embassy moved a few years later, she entertained the cream of English society and the most high ranking statesmen and diplomats. Power behind the scenes was an obsession with her; she believed she could sway the opinions of men like the Duke of Wellington, Lord Castlereagh, Canning and Lord Palmerston to look favourably on Russia's ambitions in Europe and with this purpose in mind, her entertainments at Ashburnham House were devised with the utmost ingenuity. When she gave a ball there, coloured lamps glittering like jewels were concealed among the flowers, and the background of the garden on Hay Hill was hung with a transparent landscape of moonlight and water, which became a real cascade flowing between the mossy paths and the Arcadian groups of scented shrubs. She knew exactly how to titillate the most jaded appetite for pleasure among those who were bored with too many parties every night of the Season; but she thought the English were fundamentally stupid and in spite of her Continental finesse, was never quite clever enough to realize that some of them saw through her in the end and that 'petting' the Duke of Wellington did not alter his final opinion of her as 'a *femme d'esprit*, who can and will betray everybody in turn if it should suit her purpose'.

Ashburnham House was demolished in 1899 and almost all the opulent aristocratic houses of Mayfair, which glittered all through the Season with balls and fêtes and soirées, have now gone or been converted to other uses. Flats, hotels and offices occupy the sites of Devonshire House, Londonderry House, Landsdowne House and Chesterfield House; only Bath House, built in 1821, remains in private ownership behind its high wall in Piccadilly. Burlington House was altered in 1817 and again some sixty years later; but Albany, the original Melbourne House taken over by the Duke of York and then converted into very high-class chambers by Henry Holland in 1803, retains all the charm and the exclusiveness of the

Regency and Crewe House in Curzon Street still stands in its leafy garden.

Apsley House—also known as No. 1 London, being the first large mansion at the beginning of the built-up area beyond the Hyde Park Corner turnpike—is now the Wellington Museum; and here the great Duke's collection of paintings, plate and porcelain and his military trophies, orders and decorations can be seen, as well as the dressing-case he took with him on all his campaigns with its pill-boxes, razors and ivory-handled toothbrushes. The house was originally designed by Robert Adam for Baron Apsley, afterwards Earl Bathurst, and was bought by Lord Wellesley, the Duke of Wellington's elder brother, in 1805. Lord Wellesley sold it to the Duke in 1817 and ten years later the Duke began making extensive alterations to it under the direction of Benjamin Wyatt.

Wyatt extended the structure to the west by building the Waterloo Gallery on the first floor and the rooms below it, added the Corinthian portico to the outside and refaced the whole of the exterior in Bath stone. But the Duke complained bitterly of the expense. 'I never saw him so vexed or so annoyed,' his intimate friend Mrs Arbuthnot reported. 'He said the shame and ridicule of being so cheated and imposed upon, and the having been led on to an expenditure which must ruin his family, made him quite miserable.' Wyatt, in fact, was no better than Nash at keeping to his original estimate; his final account for the alterations came to £42,000 instead of £14,000. None the less, his sumptuous decoration of the Waterloo Gallery was a brilliant revival of the eighteenth century taste of Louis XIV of France and set a new fashion which lasted for many years. It made a splendid setting for the Waterloo Banquet the Duke gave every year on the anniversary of the battle and Mrs Arbuthnot thought 'nothing could be finer or better done'. But she was mortified when the Duke decided to hang the walls with yellow damask instead of red. She thought it was 'just the very worst colour he can have for pictures' and would kill the effect of the gilding. Not that it was any use trying to argue with the victor of Waterloo. 'He *will* have it,' she wrote in her journal, and the red damask was not hung until many years later, after his death.

While the Duke was being obstinate about the renovations to Apsley House, the whole character and design of Hyde Park Corner was changing. Mrs Arbuthnot's husband, a member of Lord Liverpool's Government with considerable influence, having noticed 'the pleasing composition' of young Decimus Burton's design for

Fig. 27 *Hyde Park Corner* (Photo: A. F. Kersting)

Clarence Terrace in Regent's Park, had recommended the Office of Works to commission him for a scheme of improvement in Hyde Park. The intention was to bring the Park within the orbit of Buckingham Palace, with new drives and pathways and elegant lodges at each of the several gates, and a monumental crossing to the Green Park at Constitution Hill; and with this purpose in mind, Burton designed the graceful Ionic screen (*Fig. 27*) with a triple gateway into Hyde Park and the 'Pimlico' or Wellington Arch as the entry to the Green Park. Both have suffered aesthetically from the traffic reorganization at Hyde Park Corner, which has destroyed the scale and the harmony of Burton's original conception with the horizontal emphasis on the screen acting as a foil to the vertical emphasis of the arch; but even in Burton's own lifetime there were difficulties. The arch, modelled on the Arch of Titus in Rome, was never finished—

71

the rough panels of masonry prepared for the sculptural trophies can still be seen; and to Burton's horror, a very bad equestrian statue of the Duke of Wellington was erected on top of it, which was not removed until 1883 when the arch was resited at the top of Constitution Hill and finally ornamented by Adrian Jones's figure of Peace driving a chariot.

Sculptors and painters who pestered the Duke of Wellington to sit for them, were not popular with him. But another statue, which he could see from the windows of Apsley House, was erected in his honour in 1822 on a knoll in Hyde Park and dedicated to him and his brave companions by 'his grateful countrywomen'. This was the colossal bronze figure of Achilles by Sir Richard Westmacott, cast from the French cannon taken at Salamanca, Vittoria, Toulouse and Waterloo, which still dominates the rising ground by the new one-way traffic system through the Park. Mrs Arbuthnot admired it greatly; the Duke himself was not quite so enthusiastic. He disliked anything in the way of adulation and fuss and was repeatedly embarrassed by his wife's lack of tact in gushing over him in front of other people. Indeed, her emotional temperament and her foolishness annoyed him excessively and his home life at Apsley House was constantly bedevilled by her tiresomeness, so that he was glad to escape into Mrs Arbuthnot's drawing-room, finding her hero-worship more restrained and stimulating. He could not, of course, avoid being recognized wherever he went and his tall, upright figure, whether he was taking his morning ride in the Park or going down to the House of Lords, was a familiar sight to everyone.

High society in the Regency made Hyde Park their rendezvous at the fashionable hour of five o'clock in the afternoon (*Fig. 28*). 'The men were mounted on such horses as England alone could then produce,' according to Captain Gronow, 'and the carriage company consisted of the most celebrated beauties, amongst whom were remarked the Duchesses of Rutland, Argyll, Gordon and Bedford and Ladies Cowper, Foley, Heathcote, Louisa Lambton, Hertford and Mountjoy. The most conspicuous horsemen were the Prince Regent (accompanied by Sir Benjamin Bloomfield); the Duke of York and his old friend Warwick Lake; the Duke of Dorset on his white horse; the Marquis of Anglesea, with his lovely daughters; Lord Harrowby and the Ladies Ryder; the Earl Sefton and the Ladies Molyneux; and the eccentric Earl of Morton on his long-tailed grey .... You did not see in those days,' Gronow added, 'any of the lower or middle classes of London intruding themselves in regions which,

Fig. 28 *Hyde Park at the fashionable hour of five o'clock. By H. Alken*
(Mansell Collection)

with a sort of tacit understanding, were then given up exclusively
to persons of rank and fashion.'

The gentlemen vied with each other in being well mounted and
thought nothing of spending 1,000 guineas on a thoroughbred at
Tattersall's, the auctioneers near Hyde Park Corner, or, if they were
hard up, of hiring a good horse from the obliging Mr Tilbury, whose
high-class livery stables were in Mount Street. The ladies drove out
in superbly appointed carriages, attended by powdered footmen in
gorgeous liveries and bewigged coachmen with three-cornered hats
and French gloves. Some favoured the smart carriage known as a
vis-à-vis, designed to hold only two persons; and they were not all
duchesses or ladies of rank, though half the dukes of England and all
the fashionable young lords who were rich enough to enjoy their
charms could be numbered among their lovers. For Hyde Park was
also the hunting-ground of the professional courtesans variously
known as the 'Fashionable Impures' or Cyprians, and by such
individual names as the Mocking Bird, the Venus Mendicant, Brazen
Bellona and the White Doe, who had 'money in the funds and reclined
on the velvet cushions of Independence'.

Harriette Wilson was the starriest of them all and the idol of the
masculine half of the *beau monde*. She was born in Mayfair in a small
house in Shepherd Market (now demolished) and at the age of fifteen,

73

ran off with the Earl of Craven, whose house in Charles Street (No. 16) still stands. She quickly got tired of his curious efforts to amuse her by 'drawing cocoa trees on the best vellum paper' and gravitated into the arms of Lord Melbourne's eldest son, the Hon Frederick Lamb. But he kept her short of money in a small house in Somers Town and she was rescued by the Marquis of Lorne, later Duke of Argyll, 'an amiable, thoughtless man, who whistled away the cares of life' and was exceedingly rich. Argyll boasted among his friends of his conquest and before long Harriette's wit and her vitality had brought her to the very top of her profession.

She had bright auburn curls, tiny hands and feet, a small waist and a voluptuous bosom; and she was so popular, when she drove in Hyde Park in her carriage lined with pale blue satin, a crowd of horsemen trotted beside her, hungry for a smile of recognition or a nod, if nothing more. She could afford to be fastidious, to stand on her dignity and refuse the importunities of anyone she disliked. The handsome Lord Ponsonby, whose town house was in Curzon Street, adored her, and the Marquis of Worcester, heir to the Duke of Beaufort, caused a frightful rumpus in his family by wanting to marry her before he came of age. When he was torn from her bosom and whisked off to the Peninsular War by his irate father, a rich sugar baker, Mr Meyler, set up house with Harriette on the New Road in Marylebone, not far from her sister Amy in York Place, whose evening parties were attended by all the dandies and the foreign gentlemen of the *corps diplomatique*, the peers of the realm and the foolish young bucks down from Oxford and Cambridge. The two sisters fought like cats between themselves and spied on each other, both hiring a separate box for the season at the King's Theatre in the Haymarket in full view of the wives of the noblemen who came round to pay their respects while the performance was going on.

A box at the Opera was the Cyprians' shop window, a means of introduction to further delight; and the amorous, idle gentlemen of the Regency were totally unashamed of their uninhibited lust for sexual pleasure. They were hell-bent on living high with an absolute disregard for the consequences. The Prince himself set the pace with his debts and his mistresses, while his brother, the Duke of York, took up with Mary Anne Clarke and rashly promised her £1,000 a month. When the money failed to materialize she started making a bit on the side by selling commissions in the army, of which the Duke was Commander-in-Chief, to support herself and her establishment, consisting of twenty servants and three chefs, who served all

Fig. 29 *The Cyprians' Ball. By Cruikshank* (Victoria and Albert Museum)

her meals up on gold plate. A public examination of her conduct led to her downfall in 1809 and to the retirement of the Duke for a while to Oatlands with his rightful Duchess, who kept a hundred pet dogs which were at least a less harmful amusement.

But London thrived on the scandalous behaviour of royalty and the upper classes. The windows of the print shops and the booksellers were filled with scurrilous cartoons. Rowlandson, the Cruikshank brothers and Gillray poked blistering fun at the goings-on in high places and crowds gathered to laugh hilariously at their topical obscenities. Lampoons and ballads, dodging the laws of libel, were hawked in the streets and sold by the hundred, their vulgarity and ferocity inflaming public opinion against their rulers. Yet the power and the privilege of the favoured few, the luxury they enjoyed and the pleasures they pursued with so much gusto, continued to flourish; and at the annual ball the Cyprians gave at the Argyle Rooms (*Fig. 29*), all the well-bred gentlemen, young and old, who had been seen at Almack's the night before, abandoned themselves to a wild orgy of delight. The demi-reps in all their finery, with plumes in their hair and satin slippers and their muslin gowns slipping from their ample shoulders, were, as one writer put it, 'an invitation to penetrate the mysteries of Cytherea' which could not be resisted. Harriette Wilson and the other 'Fashionable Impures' knew what was wanted of them and they gave it with wit and gaiety for as long as their charms would permit. None of their lovers minded very much when they grew old and dwindled into poverty. The philosophy of the exclusive upper classes in Regency London was quite empty of compassion.

75

CHAPTER SIX

Entertainment

The King's Theatre in the Haymarket as the home of the Italian opera and the ballet, was London's most fashionable centre of entertainment (*Fig. 30*). Novosielsky's great horseshoe auditorium with five tiers of boxes, a gallery and a pit, was large enough to hold some 3,300 persons and even more on 'benefit nights' when the audience overflowed on to the stage, so that on one occasion Madame Rose Didelot, the Parisian danseuse, 'in throwing up her fine muscular arms into a graceful attitude, inadvertently levelled three spectators of the first quality at one stroke'.

The boxes were sold on a subscription basis for as much as £2,500 for the season, and besides exhibiting the charms of the 'Fashionable Impures', were filled night after night with gorgeously apparalled, bejewelled ladies of the highest rank. The Duchess of Richmond and the Duchess of Argyll, Lady Melbourne and Lady Jersey were among the box-holders, the Prince Regent himself and the royal Dukes of Cumberland and Gloucester. Admission to the pit cost 10s. 6d. and here the fops and the dandies made a great nuisance of themselves while the performance was going on by strolling about to show off the cut of their new clothes, besides rattling their canes and the lids of their snuff-boxes and chattering loudly to each other without being in the least disturbed when the people in the gallery shouted at them to shut up. The management built a new foyer, 'an admirable resort for a lounge', in the hope that 'in this more remote haunt, the elegant Beau may indulge in his promenade with less interruption to the Audience and to the Artists on the Stage'. But the artists were inured to the interruptions and to the frantic excitement of their supporters, no less than to the hideous demonstrations of their detractors. They carried on willy-nilly and perhaps in compensation for the bad manners of their auditors, the leading singers—Catalani, Bianchi, Tramezzani and Naldi—demanded, and were paid, enormous sums of money.

Catalani, a temperamental virago, whose fits of rage and jealousy behind the scenes were notorious, was the highest paid *prima donna* in the world. She drew immense crowds to the King's Theatre from 1806 onwards and received £2,000 for her first season in London, besides the profits of two benefit performances and some private concerts which brought her net gains up to more than £5,000. She sang in *Semiramide* and in several of Mozart's operas, with a voice that one critic described as 'extremely rich, powerful and of great compass and flexibility', though opinions differed about her acting, another critic complaining that 'she sang with a constant smile on her face, which neither the sorrows of Cleopatra nor the misplaced love of Semiramis, could repress'. Madame Pasta, who made her London debut in 1817 and later a sensational success in Bellini's *Norma*, had greater dramatic power and a phenomenal range, for she not only interpreted Bellini's tragic heroine, but was equally successful as Cherubino in *Le Nozze di Figaro* and as Dorabella in *Così Fan Tutte*.

Fig. 30 *King's Theatre, also known as the Royal Italian Opera House* (Mansell Collection)

These operas were given at the King's Theatre in Italian and with proper attention to the composer's requirements. Elsewhere, at Covent Garden, Drury Lane and the unlicensed theatres on the fringe of central London, bowdlerized versions of *Don Giovanni* in English, with the score botched up by a music master for the benefit of a popular audience, made nonsense of Mozart's intentions. Not that English singers were incapable of holding their own against the foreigners imported from the Continent when they were given the opportunity. Elizabeth Billington, born in London of a German father, and an English mother who sang at Vauxhall Gardens, made her reputation at the San Carlo Opera House in Naples and returned to the King's Theatre in triumph. The ravishing beauty of her pure and flexible voice excited the greatest admiration; one critic of her performance in *Merope e Polifonte* which had been specially written for her by one of her Neapolitan admirers, Nasolini, described the exquisite effect of her art as 'a sublime experience', and the Prince Regent was so fascinated by her, he took to visiting the musical parties she gave at her home in Fulham.

John Braham, the English tenor, was also highly successful and compared very favourably with Tramezzani, Ambrogetti and the other singers from Italy. He had a superb voice which he used with the utmost skill and kept for years, having started his career at the age of ten by singing at a concert for the benefit of his music master, Leoni, at Covent Garden, and not retiring until he was three years off sixty. By that time he was rashly persuaded by his personal popularity to sink all his savings in the ambitious project of building a theatre of his own, the St James's in King Street (demolished 1957), which cost him £26,000 and failed from the very beginning to attract the fashionable society that still crowded into the King's Theatre a short distance away.

Braham was unlucky. His disaster coincided with a new period of splendour at the King's Theatre when the Romantic Ballet from the the Paris Opéra suddenly took London by storm and the fabulous galaxy of prima ballerinas, Taglioni, Fanny Elssler, Carlotta Grisi and Fanny Cerrito, made such an impact on the imagination of the public that all other forms of entertainment suffered a temporary eclipse. Previously ballet had been no more than an appendage to the opera, staged in a somewhat haphazard and shabby manner with a corps of ill-paid and undernourished young *coryphées* and a few celebrities from Paris, such as Armand Vestris, Lise Noblet and Fanny Bias, to dance in the *divertissements*. Maria Mercandotti, a fascinating young Spaniard with 'sable hair', a tiny waist and an exquisite figure, who had been 'adopted' by the Earl of Fife on his travels in Andalusia, made a dazzling impression on the audience at the King's Theatre in 1821; but her career was brief. Two years later she eloped with the wealthy dandy 'Ball' Hughes, married him in Scotland and settled down to a life of domestic happiness in a house in Greenwich Park, where she gave wonderful parties and was much admired for her wit as well as her beauty.

London had to wait until 1830 for the *prima ballerina assoluta* of the Romantic Ballet to make her debut. She was already famous in Europe and she had the magic of a great artist: her name was Taglioni. Quite apart from her brilliant technique and her development of the art of dancing on the *pointe*, she was unique in the classical simplicity of her style. The critics went mad about her. 'She is a wonderful being and realizes all that the most sanguine imagination can picture of the poetry of dancing!' wrote one of them. 'She is all grace,' wrote another, 'preserving in every movement the purity and delicacy of an ethereal being.' And the public was enthralled. 'There was a general glitter of upraised *lorgnettes* and small telescopes in the auditorium, when she floated across the stage; one of the ugliest ladies of a certain age who had been attractively noisy during the opera, held her tongue, and there was silence in the Opera House for five seconds . . . then rapturous applause.' Flowers were flung at the ballerina's feet in a shower of gratitude and the Green Room was besieged by scores of gentlemen anxious to win her favour, though doomed to disappointment; for Taglioni, closely guarded by her father and her mother, resisted all the blandishments of her rich adorers, while accepting their lavish presents and deferring to her father's business-like judgment in the matter of all her contracts. When he arranged for her to dance in St Petersburg, London lost her for a while and her greatest rival, Fanny Elssler, danced at the King's Theatre instead, but on her return from Russia, the enthusiasm of the public was unabated.

Fanny Elssler's gifts lay in her dramatic power. She excelled in the passionate portrayal of character, 'blending the talents of the danseuse and the pantomimist with an astonishing perfection'. This again was a new development in the art of the ballet, strongly in-fluenced by the Romantic movement in literature, especially by the novels of Sir Walter Scott, and leading to a much better staging of the ballets at the King's Theatre, with elaborate settings by the talented stage designer, William Grieve. The frenzied excitement of

79

their several admirers increased the rivalry between Elssler and Taglioni and was further intensified when Carlotta Grisi made her debut in London in 1836 at the age of sixteen.

Opera and ballet were also performed during the Regency at Covent Garden and Drury Lane, but as a sideline; for these two theatres still enjoyed a monopoly in the legitimate drama, dating from the royal patents granted by King Charles II to Sir William Davenant and Thomas Killigrew in 1660. Both theatres were burnt to the ground in 1808 within a few months of each other and rebuilt almost immediately. Smirke designed and built Covent Garden in less than twelve months with a Greek Doric portico (*Fig. 31*) as the main feature of the Bow Street façade, which was also ornamented with a frieze carved by the English sculptor, John Flaxman. This frieze was all that survived the second fire in 1856 and was incorporated by E. M. Barry into the façade of the present Royal Opera House. But Smirke's handsome building cost a great deal more than the management, then under the direction of Mrs

Fig. 31 *Theatre Royal, Covent Garden. By T. H. Shepherd, 1828*
(Hulton Picture Library)

Siddons's brother, John Philip Kemble, had anticipated. More than £300,000 had been spent on the construction and the furnishings of the auditorium and to meet these severe expenses, an increase in the prices of the boxes and the pit was announced for the opening night on 18 September 1809. Catalani had been invited to sing and Kemble himself appeared with Mrs Siddons in *Macbeth*, but neither was allowed a hearing by the furious public demanding a return to the Old Prices. 'Amidst volleys of hissing, hooting and catcalls, the play proceeded in pantomime; not a word was heard save now and then the deeply modulated tones of the incomparable Siddons.' And this was only the first demonstration. Night after night for three months on end the O.P. riots went on in the new theatre, until finally Kemble had to submit.

It was not a very auspicious beginning. Mrs Siddons (*Fig. 33*), still a commanding figure with dark locks and eagle eyes and a voice that 'raised tragedy to the skies', was weary of her arduous life in the theatre after more than forty years of acting, and in 1812 she decided to retire to her new home in Upper Baker Street over-looking Regent's Park. Kemble was in debt and his supremacy as a classical actor seriously challenged in 1814 by the startling appearance of Edmund Kean at Drury Lane. Opera, Shakespeare, ballet—almost everything was tried at Covent Garden in the hope of filling the house, including an English version of Mozart's *Don Giovanni* on the same bill as *Hamlet* one evening in 1817, a revival of *The Beggar's Opera* with the bewitching Eliza Vestris displaying her elegant legs in the role of Macheath and an adaptation of Rossini's *Il Barbiere di Siviglia*. Charles Kemble, none the less, inherited an accumulation of debts when he took over the theatre from his elder brother and never succeeded in clearing them off, in spite of a few isolated successes such as Weber's opera *Oberon* sung by John Braham, Mary Anne Paton and Vestris, and the appearance of his own fifteen-year-old daughter, Fanny, in *Romeo and Juliet* in 1829.

Drury Lane, meanwhile, had not reopened after the fire until 1812. The rebuilding was entrusted to Benjamin Wyatt, whose exterior elevation has survived, though altered in 1820 by the addition of the portico designed by James Spiller and by the Ionic colonnade on the north side built by Samuel Beazley in 1831. Wyatt's auditorium, which was never very satisfactory, was swept away in 1922, but his domed Corinthian rotunda (*Fig. 32*) approached by a splendid double staircase from the vestibule still exists as the only example of the interior of a Regency theatre now to be seen in London.

Financially the new Theatre Royal was no better off than Covent Garden, Sheridan's management of the old theatre and his utter disregard of all his obligations having encumbered the shareholders with debt. The dominance of Siddons and Kemble at the rival theatre had also reduced the audiences at Drury Lane to a trickle of unfashionable nobodies. Mrs Glover, though a useful actress in comedy, was really no match for Mrs Siddons: her features, as one critic remarked, were 'too round, too sleepy and too little marked for tragedy'; and the new board of directors, which included Lord Byron and Samuel Whitbread, the brewer, were in great distress when they took a chance on the engagement of Edmund Kean.

He was the exact opposite of Kemble in every way. A little man, morose and ugly, nursing a grievance against society for the cruel years he had spent in the provinces as a strolling player battling against poverty and lack of recognition. Yet 'the fire of the Gods burned within him' (*Fig. 34*). On the stage his mean stature was transformed

Fig. 32 *Theatre Royal, Drury Lane* (Photo: Country Life)

Fig. 33 *Sarah Siddons. By Thomas Lawrence* (Hulton Picture Library)

Fig. 34 *Edmund Kean* (Hulton Picture Library)

by word and gesture, and his eyes—'those black eyes, so fierce and frightful, so tragic and so melting in their expression'—had the power to hypnotize an audience. Each well-worn character he portrayed, whether Shylock, Richard III or Iago, became a sudden, vivid revelation of the pity and the terror of the human heart; for Edmund Kean was modern and original, and in his scornful disregard of theatrical convention, the creator of a new style in acting. Hazlitt, then the dramatic critic of the *Morning Chronicle*, was one of the first to respond to his genius and to assert that 'no actor had come out for many years at all to equal him'. Coleridge declared that to see him act is like reading Shakespeare by flashes of lightning', and his success was fantastic. Playgoers fought to get into the theatre; Lady Holland invited him to dine at Holland House and all London was anxious to entertain him. But he was moody and arrogant and failed to shine in fashionable company, preferring to forget his past humiliations among his boozing companions in the low-class taverns around Drury Lane,

83

where he could behave as badly as he chose. Though well-meaning friends tried to save him from himself by good advice, his megalomania and his pride were quite beyond their understanding and no one could prevent him from dissipating his talents in drink, to the detriment once again of the financial stability of the theatre.

Besides this and the fickleness of the public, the constant financial ups and down of the two major theatres at Drury Lane and Covent Garden were further aggravated by competition from the minor theatres, licensed only to perform pantomime, farce and musical pieces, but affording a great deal of popular entertainment. The most daring venture of this kind belonged to that dazzling, debonair actress of the Regency, Eliza Vestris (*Fig. 35*), who 'sang like an angel, danced like a sylphid and possessed the most shapely legs in the world'. Her brilliant comedy and dashing appearance in the breeches parts she played with such abandon, had enlivened the theatrical scene in London for more than fifteen years, and she was

Fig. 35 *Eliza Vestris. By S. Lover* (National Portrait Gallery)

Fig. 36 *Sadler's Wells Theatre, Islington, in 1813* (Hulton Picture Library)

still at the height of her career when she suddenly decided to launch out on her own as the first woman ever to become a stage director. With all the odds against her, she bravely took over the Olympic, a small theatre in Wych Street off Drury Lane, built originally out of the deck and the wooden walls of an old French warship sold off as a naval prize soon after the battle of Trafalgar and bought by Astley, the circus proprietor.

The Olympic had failed under Astley, succeeded for a time under the eccentric actor, Elliston, and was now utterly transformed by Madame Vestris. She stretched silk across the ceiling to hide the tin roof, redecorated the ramshackle auditorium and rearranged the lights so that they would be more becoming to the ladies in the boxes. Then with a licence to produce *burletta*, extravaganza and farce, and with the help of the gifted French writer, J. R. Planché, she set to work on her productions, which for gaiety and wit, for elegance and beauty, quite outclassed the dull décor and costumes to be seen elsewhere and at once attracted a fashionable audience to the Olympic. Vestris insisted on perfection in every detail, on proper rehearsals and a more natural style of acting among the members of her company;

85

and by the freshness and originality of her approach to the art of the theatre, she made a revolutionary step forward. But her productions were costly and her haphazard, over-generous business methods, combined with her marriage *en second noce* to the extravagant, brilliant young actor, Charles James Mathews, who joined her company in 1835, brought her into the bankruptcy court, from which, however, she emerged undaunted to become the lessee of Covent Garden after Queen Victoria's accession to the throne.

Meanwhile, in the suburbs, any number of minor theatres cropped up and fell by the wayside, or like Sadler's Wells and the Surrey Theatre enjoyed great popularity all through the Regency. Sadler's Wells (on the site of the present theatre) stood among the tall poplar trees on the edge of the village of Islington (*Fig. 36*). Having once been a fashionable spa, it was now a favourite resort of the middle classes, providing them with melodrama, farce, comic opera and pantomime all through the season from Easter until the autumn. And it was here that Joseph Grimaldi, the greatest clown of all time (*Figs. 37 & 38*), made his reputation before going on to Drury Lane and Covent Garden to star in the Christmas pantomime until 1828, when he became so crippled from the many accidents he had suffered tumbling about the stage that he was forced to retire.

Grimaldi was a genius. The son of old Grimaldi and his young mistress, an English dancer at Drury Lane named Brooker, he began his career before he was three years old and was trained as an acrobat, a juggler, a swordsman, a dancer, a singer and a serious mime, so that 'every limb of him had a language'. Moreover, the clowning he invented as he grew up was unique. He changed the whole pattern of the Harlequinade, giving the Clown more prominence than the other characters drawn originally from the Italian *commedia dell'arte*, and winning the heart of his audience by the sheer magic of his humour. His bodily contortions and facial grimaces were only a part of his extraordinary capacity for making them roar with laughter or cry with him, for his gentle, lovable personality shone through all his uproarious comic business and he was generous in bestowing his gifts on the public. He sent them home refreshed and happy, though quite unaware of the cost to himself in physical and nervous exhaustion.

Pantomime alternated at Sadler's Wells with a variety of other entertainments devised by the proprietors, Charles and Thomas Dibdin, to amuse their unsophisticated audiences. There were 'aquatic spectacles', one called *The Triumph of Neptune*, the stage being flooded from the neighbouring New Riverhead waterworks,

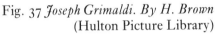

Fig. 37 *Joseph Grimaldi. By H. Brown*
(Hulton Picture Library)

Fig. 38 *Grimaldi, the clown. By H. Brown*
(Hulton Picture Library)

while a giant representation of Neptune driving the horses in his chariot wobbled somewhat uncertainly from one side of the wings to the other. Similar, though less watery, spectacles, were mounted at the Surrey Theatre and at the Royal Coburg, built in 1818 and re-opened later in the century as the Old Vic by Emma Cons and Lilian Baylis before becoming the first home of the National Theatre in 1963. But for spectacle there was nowhere like Astley's Royal Amphitheatre in Lambeth. Founded by ex-Sergeant-Major Philip Astley in 1768 as a riding school and the first Royal Circus, it was twice burnt down, and rebuilt in 1804 as 'the handsomest pleasure haunt in London'. The exterior was unimposing and most of Astley's building material, as in the little Olympic Theatre, consisted of ships' masts and spars with a canvas ceiling stretched on fir poles and lashed together with ropes. Yet the interior looked splendid and was lit by a huge chandelier containing fifty patent lamps (*Fig. 39*). Below it was the ring of sawdust, separated by the orchestra from the largest stage then known in London, framed by a proscenium arch as high as the gallery above the three tiers of boxes.

Astley's entertainments were based on horsemanship, on the superb equestrian feats of his son John and his daughter-in-law Hannah; and when Andrew Ducrow took over the Amphitheatre from the Astley family in 1824, he extended the old horseback spectacles of trick riding into 'grand military and equestrian melo-dramas', with dialogues and songs and elaborate scenes of far-fetched, romantic pageantry. Louisa Woolford, 'a gauzy and roseate dream' in the brightest of bright spangles, danced like a second Taglioni on the wide back of a white circus horse, and Ducrow himself rode his 'two wild coursers at one time at racehorse speed without saddle or bridle' round and round the ring to roars of applause. In *Mazeppa, or The Wild Horse of Tartary*, based on Byron's poem, he produced one staggering spectacle after another with a cavalcade of terrified horses galloping through a tornado of thunder, lightning and hail and all the horrors of battle, carnage and confusion against a moving panorama of

Fig. 39 *Astley's Royal Amphitheatre in 1808. By Rowlandson and Pugin*
(Mansell Collection)

the Russian steppes, before the storm-tossed hero and heroine were united in everlasting joy. *Buonaparte's Invasion of Russia* was equally hair-raising in its excitements and a representation of *The Battle of Waterloo*, with no lack of gunpowder and shot and two hundred horses in action, vied with the open-air spectacle on this same theme at the nearby Vauxhall Gardens.

Vauxhall had some advantage over Astley's in the splendour of its outdoor firework displays, enhanced by the delectable surroundings of the gardens reaching down to the river. A certain Madame Saqui of Paris, who ascended a rope to the top of the firework platform and descended again 'in a shower of Chinese fire' inspired one versifier to extol her perfections as:

> Amid the blaze of meteors seen on high
> Ethereal Saqui seemed to tread the sky!

And as time went on, more and more exotic entertainments were devised to encourage a high attendance from the public. Ramo Samee, the Indian Juggler and Sword Swallower, made a dramatic appearance in 1822, some of the ladies who watched him, fainting with admiration. Twenty thousand additional lamps were hung among the trees, and the concerts enlivened by the singing of John Braham, Kitty Stephens and the irresistible Vestris herself, whose rendering of *Cherry Ripe* caused a sensation and was sung or whistled in the streets by half the population of London. In the daytime and at night there were daring balloon ascents by the intrepid Mr Graham and his still more courageous spouse, who 'shared the perilous honours of the sky' with him, while the spectators on the ground waved and cheered.

The upper and the lower classes mingled together quite freely at Vauxhall and even more so in the arenas of sport, the bucks and the bloods of the Regency sharing their passion for pugilism and rough boxing with the *hoi polloi*. The aristocrats were proud to be seen hobnobbing with the celebrated 'bruisers' of the day—Tom Cribb and Belcher, Savage Shelton and the terrible Randall, Ned Turner, Tom Spring, Gully and the Chicken, the Gas-man and Bill Neate; and sometimes they turned their own drawing-rooms into a sparring ring. Byron took lessons from Gentleman Jackson, the ex-champion of England, at his rooms in Bond Street and was a constant spectator of the fights at the Fives Court in St Martin's Street, the Thatched House Tavern in St James's and Daffy's Club at the Castle Tavern in Holborn. Colossal sums of money were wagered in the ring and the enthusiastic crowds, drawn to the big events taking place within a few miles of the capital, often ended in fighting each other in a punch-drunk orgy of violence.

Cricket, also, was bedevilled by the craze for gambling. 'Just in front of the Pavilion at Lord's, at every great match, sat men ready with money down to give and take the current odds upon the play.' But Thomas Lord and his wealthy patrons who founded the Marylebone Cricket Club, did much to improve the standards of the game by revising the laws and laying down the general principles, which have since been observed throughout the world. Lord moved his first ground from Dorset Square to North Bank, St John's Wood, at the beginning of the nineteenth century, only to be ousted from there by Nash's proposal for cutting the Regent's Canal right through the site, which meant moving again—for the last time—to the present ground in the winter of 1813/14. Lord took his turf with him and hired a flock of sheep to crop the grass over the week-end, though according to one famous player, it was 'all ridge and furrow, resembling a billiard-table only in respect of its pockets'.

It was another thirty years before South London got its equivalent cricket ground at the Oval, laid out on part of the market gardens at Kennington. But Kennington Park and Regent's Park both provided another open-air attraction that eventually displaced the menagerie at the Tower of London. The Zoological Gardens in Regent's Park were laid out first, as an addition to Nash's original plan for the Park, the committee of the newly formed Zoological Society headed by Sir Stamford Raffles and Sir Humphry Davy, promising the Crown Commissioners that 'our buildings would be for the most part low and in no case offensive', but receiving some opposition from the inhabitants of the Park, who were doubtful of 'the lions, lynxes and leopards being so near in their neighbourhood'. Decimus Burton was appointed architect to the Society and immediately drew up a delightful plan of terraces, aviaries, dens and ponds where the animals and birds could be inspected by the learned Fellows of the Society and by the public on the payment of 1s. (*Fig. 40*). Besides building the clock-tower, which still exists and was part of the original camel house, Burton linked the two separate portions of the gardens by the tunnel that is still in use and built a number of pavilions for the zebras, jackals, llamas and monkeys donated by the various members of the Society. The first of the elephants and the giraffes were acquired soon after the opening of the gardens in 1828 and again housed by Burton in two of his most imaginative designs, which demonstrated his extraordinary versatility and were universally admired.

Fig. 40 *The Zoological Gardens, Regent's Park* (Author's Collection)

At the Surrey Zoological Gardens in Penton Place, Kennington, founded in 1831 on the menagerie collected by a certain Mr Cross, the scientific study of the animals was rather less important than their appeal to the general public in search of entertainment. The grounds, including an ornamental lake, covered about fifteen acres and the collection of animals was very comprehensive, with 'the carnivorae contained in a curvilinear glazed building 300 ft in diameter', while other attractions were also offered to the visitors. Monsieur Julien's famous orchestra performed in the evening, outplaying the chattering of the monkeys and the roaring of the lions, and there were panoramic spectacles of great magnificence, such as a representation of Vesuvius in eruption, the Siege of Gibraltar, and Napoleon crossing the Alps. These ended in firework displays, which were fun for the human spectators, if not for the animals.

Indoors, the giant panoramic representation of London in the dome of the Colosseum in Regent's Park drew crowds of visitors. This was painted by Mr E. T. Parris, who possessed 'steady nerves, enthusiasm and perseverance' and did not in the least mind 'standing in a basket, supported by two loose poles and lifted to a great height by ropes' as he worked on his immense picture showing 'the quiet, rural and cheerful scenery' to the north of the capital, the whole of the City and 'the immense bustle and business belonging to the River Thames'. The painting was viewed from the circular galleries within the dome and took on a different aspect as people moved about and climbed from one gallery to another. But this bird's-eye view of London was nothing to the optical illusion created by the Diorama in a building on the east side of Park Square, not far from the Colosseum. Here, there were two landscapes 80 foot in length and 40 foot high, 'painted in solid and in transparency and arranged so as to exhibit changes of light and shade', while the seated spectators, slowly revolving round on a mechanical turntable, imagined the scenery itself to be in motion. The Cosmorama in Regent Street, in spite of its high sounding title, could not compete with this deceptive and exciting experience, being no more than a straightforward representation of the cities of the past; while Madame Tussaud's waxworks, exhibited first in the Strand and then in Baker Street, were also without motion, but so lifelike, Maria Edgeworth was haunted by the victims of the French Revolution with their staring eyes and tousled hair. It was, perhaps, comforting to reflect that Regency London was not Paris and that its amusements were various enough to provide something for everyone.

The Artists
and the Writers

If sport was shared in some degree by all classes, patronage of the arts belonged exclusively to the wealthy aristocracy led by the Regent himself, who not only commissioned Thomas Lawrence to paint portraits of all the victorious allied statesmen and generals for the Waterloo Chamber at Windsor, but, as George IV, endowed the British Museum with the magnificent library built up by his father and also advised Lord Liverpool's Government to purchase the Angerstein Collection of pictures as the nucleus of the National Gallery.

The Angerstein Collection was put up for sale shortly after the rich owner's death in 1823 and offers from abroad had already been received when the King intervened and pressed the Government to come to a quick decision. Lord Liverpool, unlike so many ministers when it comes to spending money on the arts, was not unsympathetic, and after some debate, thirty-eight of the pictures were bought for the sum of £57,000 and put on exhibition at Mr Angerstein's former home at 100 Pall Mall. In the same year, Sir George Beaumont, another distinguished patron of the arts, offered to bequeath his own valuable collection to the nation and these paintings were also deposited in Pall Mall, causing such congestion on the walls that before long it became necessary for a new building to be acquired or erected for the purpose of housing them.

A site was chosen on the north of the new square at the top of Whitehall, which had been mapped out by Nash some years earlier to complete his grand design for the improvement of the metropolis from Regent's Park through Regent Street to Westminster. As a preliminary he had already extended Pall Mall eastwards from the Haymarket and Suffolk Street (*Fig. 41*), and had disencumbered the church

93

H

of St Martin-in-the-Fields from the shabby little houses surrounding it, remodelling the north side of the Strand with a clever arrangement of stuccoed, circular pavilions (future uncertain) to disguise the awkwardness of the angles. The north of the square was still occupied by the old Royal Mews and Nash himself designed none of the new buildings that face on to it, but Trafalgar Square, as it was eventually called when the Nelson Column was added in 1840, was yet another example of his genius for town planning, and if his idea for another handsome street to link the square with the British Museum in Bloomsbury had been adopted, London would have been all the better for it.

He was, however, fully occupied with Carlton House Terrace and Buckingham Palace at this period; and it was William Wilkins, a much younger architect, who put in some drawings at the last minute and by luck and influence secured the commission for the National Gallery. Wilkins in 1825 had already designed an effective building to house the new London University in Gower Street, providing an elegant decastyle portico on a raised podium as its central feature, leading into a vestibule surmounted by a shallow dome. The National Gallery site offered a much greater challenge, which he was not altogether capable of meeting, though here again his central portico, using the columns from Carlton House then being demolished, and the steps leading up to it, show dignity as well as grace (*Fig. 42*), if

Fig. 41 *Charing Cross. Regency improvements. By T. H. Shepherd, 1827* (Hulton Picture Library)

Fig. 42 *National Gallery* (Photo: A. F. Kersting)

the extended sections on the length of the façade and the pepper-pots on the terminal pavilions are somewhat lacking in solidity.

The new building was opened in 1838, and as it housed the Royal Academy as well as the national collection, it very soon became almost as crowded as Mr Angerstein's house in Pall Mall. The visitors, who often came in merely to shelter from the rain, were anything but well-behaved, munching food and dropping their litter everywhere; and at one time 'the foetid atmosphere, the general smell and the influx of smoky air all contributed to make a Zoo of the Gallery', while many of the artists at work on their own pictures were opposed to the whole idea of a national collection of Old Masters, fearing that it might pre-judice the public against modern art and increase their difficulties.

They had enough competition as it was from Mr Christie's Auction Rooms in Pall Mall, where the picture sales encouraged the con-noisseurs of the art world to spend their money on the works of the dead instead of in support of the living. James Christie had established his 'Great Room' in Pall Mall as early as 1766, and, with his good looks, commanding presence, great eloquence and wit, had brilliantly contrived to turn his sales into a fashionable entertainment as well as a highly profitable concern. During his lifetime he handled almost all the great pictures that came on the market and after his death in 1803, his son John James was equally successful, moving twenty years later to larger premises in King Street, St James's, on the site of the present Auction Rooms, where vast sums of money continue to be spent on all kinds of works of art. John James was as shrewd as his father and kept ahead of his rivals as the first picture dealer in London to achieve an international reputation.

The artists struggling to make a living from their work had some reason to feel aggrieved. They were almost wholly dependent on the whims of their rich patrons and had little chance of showing their paintings, except at the annual exhibition of the Royal Academy, first at Somerset House and then in Trafalgar Square. These exhibitions, moreover, were crowded beyond belief and dominated by the Academicians themselves, often at the expense of the talented and original men of genius like Constable. Benjamin West, the President until 1820, had his favourites and the hanging committee could be manipulated by intrigue, so that much jealousy and animosity was generated among those who complained of their paintings being 'skied' or hung so high that no one could see them properly, or placed so close together that one canvas glared obtrusively beside another (*Fig. 43*).

Thomas Lawrence, as the leading portrait painter of his generation, was the only artist comparatively immune from the squabbling that went on among his fellow Academicians. His extraordinary precocity as a young man brought him instant fame at the age of eighteen when he exhibited two portraits at the Royal Academy and was honoured by the high praise of Sir Joshua Reynolds. Society took him up and never lost confidence in him. He showed his patrons as they wanted to be seen—rich, elegant and rather flashy—'expressing with truth the human heart in the traits of the countenance', in the parted lips, the dilated, brilliant eyes and the profusion of sable curls falling on the pale, high forehead of his sitters. Mrs Siddons and her two daughters, with each of whom he was in love at different times and with their mother also, was one of his first inspirations; and when the Regent commissioned him to paint all the allied generals, he made a triumphant progress round the Continent, becoming an international

Fig. 43 *Exhibition at the Royal Academy in 1821. By I. R. and G. Cruikshank* (Victoria and Albert Museum)

figure at the Courts of Europe by exhibiting all his charm as well as his pictorial skill. He was knighted in 1815 and elected President of the Royal Academy in 1820 after the death of Benjamin West. Yet in spite of making a great deal of money from his portraits, he was always in debt and when he died in 1830, his superb collection of old master drawings, offered to the nation at a very low price and refused, had to be sold off to the highest bidder and dispersed.

No other portrait painter in the Regency enjoyed the success of Lawrence, but the eighteenth century fashion for portrait busts in stone continued to enrich the sculptors of the early nineteenth century. Joseph Nollekens, at the age of seventy-six, was still exhibiting at the Royal Academy in 1814, having in his time sold more than two hundred busts of Charles James Fox and William Pitt, besides carving several of the tombs still to be seen in Westminster Abbey and accumulating a fortune of £200,000. John Flaxman, after studying in Italy, devoted himself to the huge neo-Classical monuments in St Paul's to Sir Joshua Reynolds, Lord Nelson and other great public figures, and was closely associated with Sir John Soane in the making of his museum. He was professor of sculpture at the Royal Academy Schools until his death in 1826, when he was succeeded by Sir Richard Westmacott, another exceedingly prosperous sculptor working in the neo-Classical tradition, whose

97

Fig. 44 *J. M. W. Turner. By*
Charles Martin (National
Portrait Gallery)

monument to Fox in Westminster Abbey showed the statesman being
supported by Liberty with the figures of Peace and a liberated Negro
at his feet. Sir Francis Chantrey, six years younger than Westmacott,
also made a fortune out of his pompous portrait busts and oversize
statues of the dead and the living, bequeathing the sum of £150,000
to the Royal Academy at his death for the purchase of 'works of Fine
Art of the highest merit executed in Great Britain'.

Finding the right patron was infinitely more difficult for the artists
who were not interested in portraiture or in the dull repetition of the
academic style of painting. Turner (*Fig. 44*), born in Maiden Lane,
Covent Garden, the son of a barber and a butcher's daughter, the
latter with an ungovernable temper, was successful enough as a
water-colourist at the outset of his career and with his first oil paintings conceived in the classical harmony of Claude and Poussin. But as
his work developed a more individual character, thoroughly Romantic
in feeling, he was bitterly attacked by Sir George Beaumont, who
called his landscapes 'pictures of nothing, and very like'. Beaumont
failed utterly to understand both his originality and the magical effects
of light and colour he sought to achieve in his evocation of the wildest
and most excessive moods of nature.

Fortunately Turner continued to pursue his own vision undaunted by adverse criticism; and in the Earl of Egremont, the rich and eccentric owner of Petworth House in Sussex, he found a friend and a patron who recognized his genius and gave him unlimited freedom to paint some of his finest landscapes and interior scenes. As a privileged guest with his own studio in one wing of the house, Turner's erratic and self-absorbed temper was tolerated with affection by the Earl and he was in the habit of spending months on end at Petworth, where another visitor described him as 'bearing a strong resemblance to a prosperous master-carpenter, with his lobster-red face, twinkling, staring grey eyes, white tie, blue coat with brass buttons . . . turned-up boots, large fluffy hat and enormous umbrella'. He made no attempt 'to behave like a gentleman'; and in London it was said that he showed 'no faculty for friendship', being lonely, secretive, sharp-tongued and notoriously mean with his money. Other artists kept their distance from him and his house at 23 Queen Anne Street, where he lived alone from 1811 until his death forty years later, was neglected and cluttered with nearly 300 oil paintings and over 19,000 watercolour sketches and drawings, some of them so damp and dirty they fell to pieces when his executor, John Ruskin, picked them up.

Quite different in temperament and in his approach to nature was Turner's most gifted contemporary, John Constable. Born and bred under the windy skies of Suffolk with a passionate love of the country on the banks of the Stour and a passionate hatred for all that was false and 'prodigious' in the art of his time, Constable was gentle, affectionate and generous to a fault. Sir George Beaumont befriended him when he first came to London, inviting him to his house in Grosvenor Square to copy the paintings by Claude in his collection and entertaining him to dinner. But Sir George's eighteenth century taste was too narrow for him to be able to comprehend the freshness and the startling originality of Constable's innovations as a landscape painter; and although they never became enemies, it was the artist's other and less wealthy friend, John Fisher, to whom he wrote, saying: 'I have no patron but yourself—and you are not the Duke of Devonshire, or any other great ass. You are only a gentleman and a scholar and a real lover of art.'

Full recognition of his genius never really came to Constable in his lifetime; the delicate luminosity of his painting was too subtle and too far in advance of the public taste for his extraordinary gifts to be properly appreciated. And he disliked the ill-natured bickering of his fellow artists, their bitterness towards each other and the incompetent

Fig. 45 *Admiral's House, Hampstead.*
By John Constable (Tate Gallery)

administration of the Royal Academy, though Joseph Farington, an undistinguished Academician, with great influence in that august institution, eventually got him elected an A.R.A. in 1819. Farington lived in Fitzroy Square, then the artists' quarter in London and Constable rented a studio nearby in Charlotte Street; but his ardent love of the country often made him homesick for Suffolk and his only compensation when he could not go so far away was in the charming little cottage he took his wife and family to in Hampstead in the summer of 1821. At first they lodged at No. 2 Lower Terrace and later found another house in Well Walk, which delighted them both and was big enough to contain their seven young children. 'Our little drawing-room commands a view unequalled in Europe—from Westminster Abbey to Gravesend!' he wrote to Fisher. 'The dome of St Paul's in the air realises Michael Angelo's idea on seeing that of the Pantheon—"I will build such a thing in the sky!"' And the sky over the Heath was Constable's constant joy as a painter, in the wind and the rain and the noble cloud effects he never became weary of studying and sketching (*Fig. 45*). 'Independent of my *jobs*', he reported to Fisher, 'I have done some studies and made many skies and effects.... And there was one day in October so lovely that I could not paint for looking. My wife was walking with me all the middle of the day on the beautiful Heath.'

Hampstead Heath still wears the aspect of Constable's time and both his houses have survived; only the view of St Paul's has been thoughtlessly destroyed by the hideous post-war packing-cases built in the City, which now surround the glorious dome in the sky with their monstrous vulgarity. The pleasant village on the rural fringe of London, which had once been a fashionable spa in the eighteenth century, was noted for its sweet air and its beautiful situation. Keats, when he first came to live there, enjoyed walking over to Lord Mansfield's house in Ken Wood, or down the hill across the fields to Lisson Grove in Marylebone to spend the evening with Haydon, 'spouting Shakespeare' until they were both intoxicated with joy and had inspired each other with a high degree of hopefulness.

Haydon was bumptious, neurotic and a roaring egotist. When he could not ignore his difficulties or his debts, he blamed everyone else for them, and especially the established system of patronage in the arts. He had come to London in 1804 to study at the Royal Academy Schools and as a student had made friends with David Wilkie, who introduced him to Lord Mulgrave and Sir George Beaumont in the hope of furthering his career. But his grandiose ideas of his own potentiality as a history painter in the manner of Raphael and the High Renaissance militated against him and he very soon ran foul of his patrons, filling his diary with caustic reflections on their stupidity and vilifying the whole set-up of the Royal Academy under Benjamin West's presidency.

Driven by an insatiable need to prove himself worthy of his own high-flown ambition, Haydon worked—and prayed—with demoniacal energy, sitting up all night over his vast canvases and drawing for eight or ten hours on end from the Greek marbles, which had been shipped to England by Lord Elgin in 1803 and were exhibited in a temporary building attached to his home in Park Lane from 1808 until 1816. Their 'breathing nature, unaffected majesty and naked simplicity' fired his imagination, and the controversy that developed over the marbles at this time, one side accusing Lord Elgin of vandalism in robbing the Parthenon and the other furiously denying that the sculptures had any artistic merit whatever, was meat and drink to his bombastic soul. While the Government haggled over the price Lord Elgin wanted for them, Haydon wrote a passionate memo in praise of them as 'the finest works of Art in the World' and was mad with rage when the Government settled for the paltry sum of £35,000, housing these priceless works of classical art in a damp shed built alongside the Townley Gallery in the old British Museum at Montagu House.

Perhaps the trustees of the British Museum were not entirely to blame. Montagu House was hopelessly overcrowded. The expansion of the Museum since its foundation in the middle of the eighteenth century had totally outrun the available accommodation. Valuable manuscripts, Greek vases, Egyptian antiquities and 'objects of learned and curious significance' vied for exhibition space with the stuffed animals and prehistoric skeletons of the department of Natural History; and it was not until George IV with royal munificence presented his father's library to the nation in 1823, that something had to be done. Government permission was finally granted for the erection of the King's Gallery and the eventual replacement of Montagu House by a new building altogether, designed by Robert Smirke, who created the now familiar southern façade of the Museum with its extensive Ionic colonnades and somewhat massive pedimented central section (*Fig. 46*).

Smirke's building was not finished until 1847—a year after Haydon had committed suicide in despair of achieving his high ambition. The Elgin marbles by then were properly housed at last. But in 1817, when they were still in their temporary quarters, Haydon took Keats to see them for the first time and the young poet was moved to ecstasy. He shared Haydon's idealistic enthusiasm and believed in his heroics in this first year of their friendship. Haydon could do no wrong; he stood apart 'upon the forehead of the age to come', animated by the spirit of Raphael; he was the apotheosis of the poet's need for a hero. They had met at Leigh Hunt's cottage in Hampstead and while Keats admired the enormous painting of *Christ's Entry into Jerusalem* which Haydon was working on, Haydon's comment on his friend's sonnet *On Seeing the Elgin Marbles* was that it contained 'as fine an image of the Poet's yearning after high feelings, as fine a Picture of restless, searching enthusiasm as any in Poetry'.

This fulsome praise gave Keats the encouragement he needed. Born in Finsbury in his grandfather's livery stables at the Swan and Hoop and orphaned at the age of fifteen, he was already in trouble with his unimaginative guardian, Richard Abbey of Walthamstow, through having abandoned his training as a surgeon in favour of a life devoted to poetry. He had settled in lodgings in Well Walk with his

Fig. 46 *British Museum* (Photo: A. F. Kersting)

two younger brothers, not far from Leigh Hunt's cottage in the Vale of Health, and it was Hunt, as editor of the *Examiner*, who had published his first sonnet in 1816. Hunt was a curious creature: a Radical in politics who had gone to prison for writing a rude article about the Regent, a prickly, ill-natured, argumentative sort of man, yet sincere in his affections and the centre of a wide circle of friends, who found his company stimulating. Keats met Shelley and a crowd of lesser writers at his home and spent many evenings alone with him, enjoying his 'matchless conversation', before walking back to Well Walk across the Heath with his head in the stars and his eyes fixed on a bright vision of the future.

But in 1818 his favourite brother Tom died of consumption and after nursing him for months on end, Keats went to live with Charles Armitage Brown, who, with another friend, Charles Wentworth Dilke, had built a charming pair of semi-detached villas in a communal garden on the lower part of the Heath near Pond Street. Known as

103

Fig. 47 *Keats House, Hampstead* (Photo: Christopher Oxford)
(Camden Borough Council)

Wentworth Place and now exquisitely arranged as the Keats Museum
(*Fig. 47*), this was the house inhabited by the poet off and on for the
rest of his life in England. It was here, in the garden, that he felt 'a
tranquil and continual joy' in the song of a nightingale and was seen
by Brown sitting under the plum tree one morning at breakfast time
with some scraps of paper in his hand, which he afterwards concealed
behind some books and which Brown discovered to be the first draft
of the rapturous *Ode to a Nightingale*. And it was here, when the
Dilkes moved away from their part of the house, that Mrs Brawne
and her three children came to live.

Fanny, the eldest, aged eighteen, was gay and fascinating, with a
fondness for parties and pretty clothes and 'for acting stylishly',
though by no means the 'ignorant little minx' Keats once called her
in a fit of pique. It was not her fault if she sometimes failed to understand the depth of his feelings or the complexity of his passionate
nature; neither was it very surprising if her family and friends disapproved of the unofficial engagement between her and her next-door-
neighbour. Keats was constantly in financial difficulties and his poetry

was most savagely attacked by the critics, so that it seemed he would never be in a position to marry or could only make the most imprudent husband. Moreover, his health was visibly deteriorating from the winter of 1819 all through the summer of 1820, to the time when Mrs Brawne and Fanny devoted themselves to nursing him before he finally left Hampstead for Italy with the travelling cap Fanny had lined with silk for him and a lock of her hair.

The despair and the agony that overshadowed Keats in those last tragic months at Wentworth Place were not, however, by any means the whole of his life. Before his sickness overcame him, no amount of failure or frustration ever succeeded in destroying his youthful ardour or his exuberance. And with his young friends he enjoyed all the intellectual excitements of Regency London, the acting of Kean at Drury Lane, the upsurge of the Romantic Movement in painting and poetry, the lectures of William Hazlitt, the critical essays of Charles Lamb, the literary jokes and the uninhibited horseplay they got up to among themselves. Claret was cheap and plentiful, even when money was scarce, and they borrowed off each other when funds were low, pursuing their ideals with zest and energy, walking miles through the airy fields of Hampstead, Kilburn and Islington, forever questioning, debating and arguing the meaning of life and the purpose of art. Their world was distinct from the extravagant, empty world of fashionable society at Almack's and the gambling clubs in St James's, but it flourished in its own orbit with a creative splendour that has seldom been matched at any other time.

Charles Lamb, like Keats, was a Cockney, born in Crown Office Row in the quiet precincts of the Temple. The son of a barrister's clerk with very little money, he was educated at Christ's Hospital, where he met Samuel Taylor Coleridge and formed the first of his lifelong friendships. At fourteen he became a junior clerk in the South Sea Office and two years later moved to a desk in the East India Office in Leadenhall Street, where he stayed until he was pensioned off in 1825 and 'went home—for ever'. At no time was his income more than £600 a year and from the age of twenty-one he made himself responsible for the care of his sister Mary, who in a fit of insanity had stabbed her mother with a carving knife and from time to time had to be put away in an asylum at Hoxton.

This appalling tragedy lurked in the background of Charles Lamb's marvellous affection for his sister; yet he never complained of the burden or allowed it to embitter his attitude to the rest of the world. Instead it deepened his tenderness and his human understanding, and his friends found him unique. Coleridge, Wordsworth, Hazlitt, Haydon, Hunt and Godwin might quarrel among themselves—they often did—but they never quarrelled with Lamb, or not for long. At his 'Wednesdays', the parties he gave on Wednesday evenings in Russell Street, Covent Garden, he never failed to draw everyone together in harmony. The cards for cribbage or whist were laid out on the table with a snuff-box for communal use, and a cold supper ready on the sideboard with plenty of hot punch and brandy and water to encourage 'the flight of high and earnest talk that took one half way to the stars', the whimsical laughter and the fun.

Lamb loved London. 'Covent Garden,' he declared, 'is dearer to me than any Garden of Alcinous.' And he wrote of 'the impossibility of being dull in Fleet Street, the crowds, the very dirt and the mud, the sun shining upon houses and pavements, the print-shops, the old bookstalls and the pantomimes—London itself a pantomime and a masquerade—all these things work themselves into my mind and feed me . . . and I often shed tears in the motley Strand from fulness of joy at so much Life.' Living for more than fifty years in and out of different lodgings in the Temple, in Russell Street and then in Duncan Terrace, Islington, when he finally moved out to Enfield and Edmonton after his retirement, he was miserable. 'Streets, streets, streets, markets, theatres, churches, shops sparkling with pretty faces of industrious milliners, neat sempstresses, ladies cheapening . . . lamps lit at night, pastry cooks' and silversmiths' shops, beautiful Quakers of Pentonville, noise of coaches, drowsy cry of mechanic watchmen at night, with bucks reeling home drunk'— these were the sights and the sounds that moved him. 'All these emotions must be strange to you,' he wrote in a letter to Wordsworth. 'So are your rural emotions to me.' Yet he was one of Wordsworth's greatest admirers and their friendship was never impaired by their differences of taste.

Wordsworth visited London quite often, but preferred his solitude in Westmorland and disliked the city, except in the early morning when he was crossing Westminster Bridge and saw it 'All bright and glittering in the smokeless air'. Coleridge was more restless, forever seeking a change of scene to stimulate his health and forever talking like the Ancient Mariner buttonholing the Wedding Guest, his eloquence and the extraordinary range of his intellect hypnotizing all his friends. Yet by the age of thirty he was already sinking under a thickening haze of opium. 'The poet is dead in me,' he wrote. 'My imagination lies like cold snuff on the circular rim of a brass candlestick, without even a stink of tallow to remind you that it was once clothed and mitred with flame'; and in 1806 his wife, who had never understood the fantastic flights of his genius or what he was suffering, left him for good.

Four years later a far more serious blow shattered his wavering self-esteem: Wordsworth, believing there was 'no hope for him', withdrew from the close intimacy which had so enhanced the early days of their friendship. But Lamb loved him for all time, however difficult he became, and while he was working on his brilliant lectures on literature at the Royal Institution, he found a home with the Morgans in Hammersmith. Then in 1816 he put himself under the care of Mr Gillman, an apothecary living in The Grove at Highgate, in the hope of finding some cure for his fatal weakness. 'He is very bad,' Lamb reported to Wordsworth, 'but then he wonderfully picks up another day, and his face, when he repeats his verses, hath its ancient glory; an archangel a little damaged.' Old friends and new disciples went out to the village of Highgate, climbing the long hill, to hear him talk on every conceivable subject, or just for the sound of his voice, which remained as spell-binding as ever even when his mind wandered and became confused. Mr and Mrs Gillman were unfailingly kind and patient; but the vivid young Coleridge, worshipped by his friends and idolized by Hazlitt as the most inspiring prophet of his generation, had burnt himself out long before the middle-aged and befuddled drug addict died in Highgate in 1834.

His most fervent admirer, William Hazlitt, was a Londoner by adoption. The nervous, high-strung and talented offspring of a Nonconformist minister in Shropshire, he came to London at the age of fifteen to complete his education at the Unitarian College in Hackney, lodging with his elder brother in Long Acre. But the allurements of the intellectual life of the city, the theatres, the streets and the crowds drew him away from the purpose of his studies and by the time he was twenty he had married Sarah Stoddart, a friend of Charles Lamb's, and had started out on his not very successful career as a portrait painter. In 1812 he settled in London for good, turning his attention to journalism, first as parliamentary reporter and then as dramatic critic on the *Morning Chronicle*. Mrs Siddons and Edmund Kean excited his ardent enthusiasm and while increasing his devotion to the theatre, inspired him to develop his essays on the drama into an art. His *View of the English Stage* was a landmark in dramatic criticism and his lectures on Shakespeare and the English Poets expressed his fearless opinions regardless of

any offence he might give to his friends. Some of them objected
strongly and their hostility towards him helped to sour his temper,
which had already been injured by the failure of his marriage and of
his disastrous love affair with Sarah Walker, the daughter of his land-
lord at 9 Southampton Buildings. Lamb, faithful as ever in his friendship, took no notice of his sardonic moods, even accepting his most
ill-natured gibes. 'There was a cut at me some time back in the
Examiner,' he wrote, 'which the author has collected to my disparage-
ment, from some hundreds of social evenings we had spent together—
however in spite of all, there is something in my attachment to H
which these violent strainings cannot quite dislocate or sever asunder.
I get no conversation in London that is absolutely worth attending
to but his.'

Good talk was the absolute elixir of life among the literary men of
the Regency, not only in the intellectual circles of Lamb and Leigh
Hunt, but in the social sphere beyond their means. Holland House,
the turreted Jacobean mansion in the rural country of Kensington
belonging to Lord Holland, was the rendezvous of all the most distinguished Whig statesmen, scholars, men of letters and wits for a
period of more than thirty years. His lordship was cordial and kind;
his lady, who had eloped with him and married him after being divorced by Act of Parliament, more domineering, and the most assidu-
ous lion-hunter in London. She was outspoken and very caustic in
her remarks on the personal eccentricities of her guests, ticking
them off without mercy; yet everyone always returned for more
punishment, for no one dared, or wanted, to ignore an invitation to
Holland House. Friends arriving for dinner, stayed the night to
avoid going back to town in the dark, and walked with Lord Holland
in the garden the next morning. Byron, Tom Moore, Samuel Rogers
and Henry Luttrell, Sydney Smith, Sir Walter Scott and Macaulay,
as a very young man, enjoyed 'the constant flow of conversation, so
natural, so animated, so various, so rich with observation and anecdote'
in the great dining-hall and the oak-pannelled library, and they took
Lady Holland's asperities in their stride.

The banker poet, Samuel Rogers, disliked her a good deal, but
was a constant visitor to Holland House and had his favourite seat
in the garden. His own breakfast parties and dinners at No. 22 St
James's Place were lively and attractive, and his house, though small,
was full of the paintings and *objets d'art* he had been collecting for
years. His tongue could bite like Lady Holland's and his wit was
barbed with malice; yet his friends trusted him and as a host he was

incapable of being embarrassed, even when Byron on his first visit to St James's Place, refused every dish that was put in front of him and asked for biscuits and soda water when there were none in the house, making do in the end with mashed potatoes and vinegar. Not a very good poet himself, a word of praise from Rogers conferred an accolade on the literary men who sought his acquaintance and to be adopted by him as a friend was to enter the kingdom of Parnassus.

Tom Moore, an engaging young Irishman with a charming voice and a great facility for composing tuneful melodies to suit the words of his own sentimental lyrics, ingratiated himself with Rogers soon after he arrived in London and from that moment was *persona grata* with the cream of society. He was soon on very good terms with the Hollands and shared the brilliant heyday of Byron's success 'in the year of revelry 1814, at the pleasantest parties and balls all over London, warbling duets with Lady –', and although only the son of a Dublin grocer, 'entering the most aristocratic drawing-rooms with a gaiety and an ease combined with a kind of worshipping deference, that was worthy of a prime minister in the court of Love'.

Moore 'dearly loved a lord', but his snobbery in no way detracted from his delightful personality or his intellectual effervescence, and his devotion to Byron was sincere. They laughed and frollicked together and were deeply attached to each other, and after Byron had been driven to take refuge in Italy, it was to Moore that he handed over the MS of his memoirs. Moore unhappily pledged the MS to Byron's publisher, John Murray, against a loan he was badly in need of and was too honest to resist the pressure that Byron's officious executors put upon him after the poet's death, so the MS was torn up and burnt in the grate of John Murray's drawing-room in Albemarle Street in 1824 and what might have been the true story of the poet's life was lost for ever. Moore did his best to forgive Murray, but he could not forgive 'the riotous curiosity of the mob, the bustle of the undertakers and all the other accompaniments of the ceremony' at Byron's funeral. He saw 'few respectable persons among the crowd' and for once his blithe spirit was shaken—for the mob was an aspect of London that most people contrived to ignore.

CHAPTER EIGHT

The Populace

The London mob was unpredictable. It could not be pinned down, nor could its temper be judged by reason, for no one could ever be quite certain how it would react and no one knew where it came from or where it dispersed to; it simply appeared like a cloud of locusts, predatory and menacing, and then cleared off, leaving a trail of destruction behind it.

Ever since the Gordon Riots in 1780 when the city had been terrorized for days on end, successive governments had viewed the mob with suspicion and in the absence of a proper police force, could find no way of controlling it, except by calling out the Guards. Yet it was not in essence a revolutionary movement among the people. It had no acknowledged leaders and was not a cohesive group, though it could be stirred up and exploited for political purposes by men like Henry Brougham in support of Queen Caroline, or against the Duke of Wellington when much of the blame for the post-war difficulties of the nation was concentrated on him. The Duke showed his courage and his utter contempt of the rabble by continuing to ride in the Park or from Apsley House to Westminster, unattended; he had only to turn his horse abruptly and flick his whip at the hooligans for them to scatter in all directions. But he did consent to having locks fitted to the doors of his carriage and a few years later during the riots in favour of the Reform Bill, the shrieking, howling populace out for his blood, found the windows of Apsley House barred with iron shutters and two cannons from Waterloo mounted by the gateway.

It seemed as if revolution was imminent and would come as the climax to the repressive measures inflicted on the people by the Government. In fact, the Government was frightened and the people themselves were utterly bewildered by the changes wrought in

Britain through the exigencies of fighting so long a war. The new industrialism in the North, the plight of the agricultural labourers in the South, and the inflationary pressure on prices were all a consequence of the struggle to defeat Napoleon, and while the rich had become far more wealthy, the poor had become more desperate. Hundreds of starving, dispossessed agricultural workers poured into London from the countryside to mingle with the depraved inhabitants in the poorer quarters of the city. In the dark, blind alleys of St Giles's Rookery, Clare Market, Cloth Fair, Clerkenwell and the eighteenth-century slums of the East End, whole families lived like rats with a bundle of rags for a bed, no hope of any honest work and no comfort except in drink.

Gin was cheap. The lowest taverns in the metropolis (*Fig. 48*) offered to make a man drunk for a penny and dead drunk for two-pence, with free straw to lie on and sleep off the effects. And this was a luxury, an irresistible temptation. Small children were sold off to the chimney-sweeps as 'climbing boys' for a few pounds that could be spent on gin. Pawnbrokers abounded in every street and alley, ready to advance a few shillings on a ragged coat stolen off the back of a

Fig. 48 *A gin shop in Covent Garden. By Cruikshank, 1821* (Mansell Collection)

drunkard in his sleep for the money to be spent on gin. More extensive thieving and prostitution yielded even better results and the men and women willing to perpetrate any sort of crime for the money to get drunk on Madame Geneva, Strip-me-naked or Blue Ruin, as this intoxicating liquor was variously called, had nothing to lose. If not sodden into a state of lethargy, they were inflamed into further violence, running wild in an orgy of destruction, breaking windows and throwing stones, chasing their victims in the streets and shouting obscenities at them. The Bow Street Runners and the parish constables were too few in number to do much about it, and it was not until Sir Robert Peel established his blue-coated Metropolitan Police in 1829 that any kind of discipline was imposed on the rotting underworld of London.

The middle classes contrived to keep out of trouble: they worked hard as clerks in the City, in the shops and as craftsmen or professional lawyers and doctors. The raffish bucks of the upper classes were not so abstemious; they met the corrupt and vicious populace on its own ground in the stews of Covent Garden and Drury Lane. Prostitutes paraded themselves in the Green Room of the two Royal Theatres in all the glory of their trumped-up finery: 'brilliant Fanny decked out with an elegant muff and dashing plume of feathers . . . fair Maria and the pretty Ellen throwing out lures . . . and lusty, black-eyed Jane

Fig. 49 *The Lobby at Drury Lane. By Cruikshank, 1821* (Mansell Collection)

with white soft arms and nature's snowy orbs well displayed' by the low cut of her muslin gown (*Fig. 49*). The top-hatted gentlemen in their waisted coats and tight pantaloons, after quizzing the ladies judiciously, offered them wine and jellies and piled them into a hackney coach driven to a secret hideout, or strolled across the once fashionable Piazza of Covent Garden with their prize and disappeared into one of the dives behind Inigo Jones's crumbling colonnades. The obscene old women seen by Hazlitt lurking in the lobby of Drury Lane in their long duffle cloaks and rusty black bonnets, with a crowd of innocent looking young girls in their clutches, acted as procuresses, filling their own fat purses at the expense of the young women they employed, and the bagnios in the district did a roaring business in satisfying the lust of Corinthian Tom and Jerry Hawthorne. The fun was anything but harmless. Flagellation, sodomy and every kind of sexual aberration could be gratified for money. Gambling, drinking and blackmail were added to the dangers of fornication, and the dissipated bucks were often to be found in the morning stripped naked of all their money and their clothes, in no condition to meet a new day when the country people from the market gardens in the suburbs arrived with their baskets of vegetables and their bundles of flowers.

Lamb found 'all the bustle and the wickedness about Covent Garden, the very women of the Town, the Watchmen, drunken scenes and rattles' amusing. Byron, tired of being fêted by society and bored with the capriciousness of Lady Caroline Lamb, went in search of depravity, only to discover that it increased his ennui. Edmund Kean descended into the Coal Hole and the notorious Cyder Cellars in Maiden Lane to carouse with the lowest dregs of the underworld before he finally drank himself to death. And the numbers of unknown, unnamed people who perished in the same way were never recorded. Some of them never emerged into the daylight at all, though the streets were as crowded in the daylight hours as at night. A seething rabble of street vendors, crippled soldiers and sailors, prostitutes, chimney-sweep boys with sores and tuberculosis, of ballad singers, midwives, quack doctors, pimps and pickpockets, was constantly on the move in the derelict areas of London and even in the elegant squares and streets of Mayfair, where they mingled with the better class inhabitants and sought to corrupt their servants or lead them into mischief.

Better lighting, paving stones for the pedestrians and a comparative lack of filth in the streets had immeasurably improved the safety and the whole aspect of the West End; but Louis Simond, a visitor to

London in 1811, was utterly shocked by the colony of Irish labourers occupying a cul-de-sac near his lodgings in Orchard Street, Portman Square, which he described as one of the finest parts of the town. 'They fill every cellar and every garret,' he wrote, 'a family to each room; very poor, very uncleanly and very turbulent. They give each other battle every Saturday night. . . . I have never heard anything similar to the noise these neighbours of ours make, in any other part of the town at any hour of the night, even in St Giles's.' And the watchmen, he noted, were terrified of interfering, one of them being heard to say: 'Never mind, let them murder each other if they please.'

Murder in these circumstances was bound to go undetected and the penalty of hanging be made inoperative, even if for once it was not too harsh a punishment. A man or a woman could be hanged for far less—for stealing a horse or breaking into a house; and although the procession of criminals to the gallows at Tyburn had at last been done away with in 1783, public executions still took place outside Newgate

Fig. 50 *Execution outside Newgate Prison* (Mansell Collection)

and were a Roman holiday for the mob as well as a spectacle enjoyed by the better classes. Every window overlooking Dance's great castellated prison was booked for these occasions by the young bloods seeking a sensation, or by the quite sober looking tradesmen and their wives, who came to watch the process of justice catching up with their less respectable brethren. The mob gathered overnight and pressed up against the barrier in front of the scaffold, growing ever thicker and more suffocating, more ribald, more ferocious and more excited as the clock on St Sepulchre's Church chimed the hours away. The pale dawn saw thousands of upturned faces (*Fig. 50*) concentrating on the black door of the prison—young, old, wrinkled and brutalized, with scowling and grinning mouths, feverish and bloodshot eyes, necks distorted by the effort of craning up, arms and bodies crushed like sausages. The fun was about to begin when the dark hangman appeared with his victim in chains, which were solemnly cut away to the abominable chorus of yells bursting from the multitude. Then a moment of silence and a human figure kicking and dangling by the neck, and the hands of the hangman appearing from a trap-door beneath the scaffold to grasp the dying ankles with a final jerk. No wonder the mob shrieked and howled like animals and turned away to look for further gratification of their most bestial instincts. It did not occur to the authorities that cruelty and a lust for blood might be aggravated, not deterred, by the public exhibition of the hangman's art.

Yet it was not always a vicious excitement that stirred the *hoi polloi*. Their exuberance and their coarse good humour found an outlet in the holiday fairs at Smithfield and at Greenwich. Bartholomew, the oldest and the biggest of all the London fairs, founded in 1133 by Prior Rahere on the open ground of West Smithfield in front of the church of St Bartholomew the Great, was still going on, though its original purpose as a trading fair had long been forgotten and the populace went there to enjoy themselves, to eat roast pig and get drunk, to view the freaks, the tumblers, the dancing pig and the theatrical entertainments at Richardson's booth (*Fig. 51*). Richardson was the most successful showman of the age. He claimed that his scenery and costumes were as good as anything to be seen at Covent Garden or Drury Lane and that many of the most eminent actors, including Edmund Kean, had made their first appearance in his travelling theatre. And he knew how to attract the public. Outside his great booth at Bartholomew Fair was a platform where the actors paraded before the performance with their drums and trumpets to

Fig. 51 *Bartholomew Fair, Smithfield. By Rowlandson and Pugin, 1808*
(Mansell Collection)

proclaim all the wonders and delights within. On the stage he produced elaborate melodramas, such as *The Wandering Outlaw*, with
the hair-raising appearance of an avenging ghost in the final scene,
followed by a comic harlequinade and a splendid panorama, with any
number of acrobatic turns in between.

Richardson had started life working for a cow-keeper in Islington
at 1s. a day and died in 1837 at the age of seventy worth £20,000. He
was illiterate, and highly irascible when his temper was roused, but
his generosity was a legend among the less successful showmen and
performers on the fairgrounds and his energy was remarkable. When
Bartholomew Fair was over at the end of August, he packed up his
booth and moved on into the provinces, reappearing at Greenwich at
Easter. Here there were stalls selling toys and trinkets, gingerbread,
oysters, whelks and gin; and besides Richardson's booth, Wombwell's
magnificent menagerie was on show, to say nothing of the dwarfs and
giants, the Merry Andrews, the man-monkey, and Toby the learned
pig, who could 'spell, read, cast accounts, tell the points of the sun's
rising and setting, and the age of any party'. Respectable people

tended to stay away from Greenwich and to complain of the noise
and the disturbance in the neighbourhood, but for the Cockney boys
and girls and bad characters of the city, the sailors and their doxies,
the Fair was an uproarious lark for three days on end.

Almost any gathering of any sort was fun and fair game for the
populace. Balloon ascents from St George's Fields on the south side
of the river drew enormous crowds of spectators. And in the Great
Frost of 1814, when the Thames between the dilapidated piers of old
London Bridge and the new Blackfriars Bridge was frozen over for
the last time, a fair was set up on the packed ice (*Fig. 52*), with booths
selling hot loaves and cuts of meat from the pigs and the oxen roasted
on the spot. Bookstalls, skittle-alleys, Punch and Judy showmen,
pedlars, hawkers of ballads, perambulating pie-men, oyster wenches
and fruit sellers appeared overnight. Brandy balls, gin, beer and
gingerbread were there for the asking and even a printing press was
assembled on the ice. No one seemed to mind the intense cold, or
they warmed themselves with hot potations and the excitement of
'pricking the garter' in the gambling booths.

The powers of survival of the Cockney populace were astonishing.
Poverty and disease, bad food and too much Blue Ruin made the
tough drama of their lives a never-ending battle against the forces of
order and decency; yet vice and corruption never quite destroyed their

Fig. 52 *Frost Fair on the Thames in 1814* (Hulton Picture Library)

boisterous energy or their positive enjoyment of the squalor they lived in, and they only joined in the Radical movement set off by the class above them because it seemed to offer them another chance of making mischief. The Radicals, nevertheless, were sincere in their earnest desire to improve the lot of the people. They were inspired by Jeremy Bentham, an elderly recluse living in Queen's Square Place, Westminster, next door to Hazlitt, who was in the habit of pointing him out to his friends as he walked in his beautiful garden, ruminating on his philosophy of 'the greatest happiness of the greatest number'. Bentham's Utilitarianism stood for the disinterested application of intelligence to social problems and was a challenge to the Establishment, though he was not in favour of revolution. He taught Francis Place, the master breeches-maker, whose premises at No. 16 Charing Cross became the headquarters of the Radicals and was known as 'the Gossip-shop of reformist politics', and he also found a most ardent young disciple in James Mill, who lived at Rodney Terrace, Pentonville, and published his reformist tract on *Government* as a sixpenny pamphlet in 1820.

James Mill believed that 'the middle rank, universally described as both the most wise and the most virtuous part of the community' should set a good example to the lower orders, and this was quite a new and adventurous way of thought, for it was only in the 1820s with the development of the Industrial Revolution and of London as the centre of a great trading nation that the opinions of the middle classes and their pressure for more representation in Parliament began to carry some weight. Not that the idealism of the Radical Movement meant very much in these early years to the illiterate men and women it was designed to assist, any more than did the writings of William Godwin, another middle-class reformist, whose abstract theories on government inspired his future son-in-law, Shelley, to ecstasies of enthusiasm. Indeed, it was Godwin's dialectics that took fire in the poet's mind and fed by his youthful ardour and his exquisite sensitivity, became a paean of praise for love and liberty as the guiding light of mankind and the corner-stone of human relations. All this and his professed atheism made Shelley an outcast from society and a dangerous revolutionary in the eyes of everyone except his most admiring friends. His interminable quarrels with his father gave him an intense feeling of persecution, and his own neurotic, undisciplined behaviour in eloping with Harriet Westbrook and then with Godwin's daughter, Mary, combined with Harriet's suicide in the Serpentine and the subsequent decision of the Lord Chancellor that he was unfit to take care of his motherless children, increased the hostile forces against him; and it was not at all as one of England's greatest lyric poets that he was regarded when he left for Italy in 1818, but as one of her most undesirable citizens and a danger to the community.

Shelley was drowned at Lerici four years later and among his friends the tragic circumstances of his death heightened the drama of his impassioned philosophy of life. But among the pot-house politicians in London and the working people themselves, his bright vision of a world without tyranny, prejudice and superstition made no impression. Love was not a word they understood and liberty was only another name for anarchy, at least in the minds of Arthur Thistlewood and his companions in the Cato Street conspiracy of 1820. Thistlewood was a seedy ex-officer of the militia, who conceived the idea of assassinating the entire Cabinet when its members were dining together at Lord Harrowby's house in Grosvenor Square, as a retribution for the distressing massacre of the Manchester cotton workers at Peterloo. He gathered a handful of thugs round him in a barn in Cato Street off the Edgware Road, arming them with swords and pistols and canvas bags for the heads of their victims, but was betrayed by one of his fellow conspirators and surprised by the Bow Street Runners on the night of February 23rd. Thistlewood ran one of the Bow Street men through with his sword before he was overpowered and rounded up with the rest of his company, all of whom were brought to the gallows some months later.

This crazy conspiracy, plotted in the very heart of London, shook the Government badly and was an excuse for still more repressive measures against the working classes. Yet most of the Radicals were in favour of peaceful pressure on the Establishment for the reforms they advocated, and they were not averse to aping the upper classes they wished to overthrow. The Radical member of Parliament, Sir Francis Burdett, was a gentleman. Henry Hunt, known as 'Orator' Hunt, pretended to be one, by dressing up in a white top hat, doeskin breeches and fine linen in the authentic mould of a Regency buck. Even William Cobbett, the red-hot political journalist, wore a swansdown waistcoat like a gentleman farmer; but he was shocked and disillusioned when 'Orator' Hunt was seen going to a mob meeting in Spitalfields with his mistress sitting beside him in his carriage. Hunt, in fact, made a grave mistake in parading his own misconduct; for many of his followers were linked to the Evangelical movement in the church and to the Nonconformist sects proliferating in London and the provinces, and they objected as much to the moral depravity of the Regent and his entourage as to the long hours and ill rewards of the working man.

Evangelical piety, propagated by the Clapham Sect and the Religious Tract Society, appealed most strongly to the middle-class inhabitants of London, whose wealth and power were on the increase. Genteel persons like William Wilberforce and Hannah More worked passionately for the redemption of souls at home and for the abolition of black slavery abroad, while the Regent and high society guzzled the rich food at their tables and piled up their gambling debts. Wesley's Chapel in the City Road, Whitefield's in Tottenham Court Road and the Lambeth Chapel, built in 1817, drew large congregations of the faithful at the same time as the gin shops and taverns were overflowing with the drink-sodden flotsam of humanity. The middle classes needed a practical creed to justify their upward progress in the world, a creed to offset the immorality of the class above them and to keep the depraved class below them in its place. Often they mistook respectability for grace and their zeal was not without a touch of humbug, but philanthropy was not a Victorian discovery; it existed already among the 'do-gooders' of the Regency and the reign of George IV and gradually assumed a wider influence over the lives of the people of London as the middle classes expanded and their self-imposed mission as reformers of society gathered pace.

Better off than they had ever been before through their own industry and application, the middle classes occupied the terraced houses in Bloomsbury, St Marylebone and Islington, or built themselves respectable villas in the new suburbs, consolidating their position as they went along and creating a new social pattern of sobriety between the very rich and the very poor. They took pride in being decently dressed without following the foibles of fashion, while remaining distinct from the ragged, disreputable appearance of the lower orders, and they studied to uphold the doctrine of James Mill by preferring virtue to self-indulgence and solid progress to excessive extravagance.

Yet the self-indulgent extravagance of the upper classes which the middle rank condemned so heartily, did not by any means always operate to the detriment of the working population. The numbers of servants required by the more ostentatious and opulent members of high society gave regular employment indoors and out to more than a third of London's inhabitants. Butlers, footmen, coachmen, gardeners, cooks, kitchen boys and female servants in the larger households were not ill-treated if they behaved themselves. Young girls fresh from the country, if not 'of a pert and saucy disposition', could work their way up to the enviable position of head housemaid or even to the higher grade of lady's maid, provided they were not tempted 'to comb their hair with their mistress's combs, make free with her threads and pins etc. or cut their corns with their master's razors'. Boys starting with the interminable odd jobs in the basement and the cellars, could aspire to the sumptuous livery of a footman in one of the patrician mansions in the West End, or to the top job of a gentleman's gentleman. It was only the Duke of Wellington who disliked too many servants fussing round him and declared that he preferred to polish his own boots.

All over London in the cobbled mews behind the Georgian terraced houses, the squares and the new Regency developments, there were stables for the horses and carriages of the well-to-do with accommodation of a sort for the coachmen, ostlers and boys, who cared for their charges with a quite extraordinary devotion. Most of these are now garages or expensive and very attractive little houses that have been modernized. But in the Regency the mania for riding and driving a smart equipage was at its zenith and to keep a good stable was a status symbol. Carriage horses were matched with the utmost care and groomed to a glossy perfection, besides being nourished and cosseted by a whole army of attendants and a vast organization of wagons bringing fodder and straw and bales of hay in from the farms and fields of Surrey and Middlesex. At Tattersall's horses were bought and sold for colossal sums of money and the sporting aristocracy mingled with the touts, the gamblers and the sharpers, meeting the same company on the racecourses outside London; for almost everyone was horse-mad and nothing brought the aristocracy more respect and admiration than their passion for horseflesh and their lavish display of an elegant coach or phaeton. When the members of the Four-in-Hand Club, Lord Worcester, Lord Sefton, Lord Barrymore, Sir John Lade and Colonel Berkeley, assembled in George Street, Hanover Square, before driving off in style to dinner at Salt Hill, half the population of London turned out to quiz each superb looking 'drag' and its team of horses and to cheer their departure.

Coach-building was a thriving industry in London. Mr Vidler of Millbank had the monopoly of building and supplying the mail coaches to the G.P.O. and was also responsible for their maintenance. Every coach that came into London in the morning bespattered with mud and thick with dust, was immediately taken back to the works at Millbank to be cleaned and greased and overhauled at a cost of 1s., before being put on the road again the same afternoon and sent off on its long journey. A large number of expert craftsmen, wheelwrights, upholsterers and harness-makers were employed at the workshop and quite a few artists to paint the door panels; for whereas machinery was taking hold in the North of England and the Midlands, craftsmanship of the highest order was still the most rewarding kind of work to be had in London.

The unhappy conditions of the Spitalfields silk weavers with no work on their hands, had not yet spread to the Whitefriars glassmakers, the Battersea enamel works or the Chelsea china factories; and there were silversmiths, goldsmiths, and jewellers in Hatton Garden, watch and clock-makers in and around Clerkenwell, precision instrument makers and gunsmiths in the Strand, and bootmakers, hatters, tailors, glove and stay-makers everywhere. New fashions in furniture using Greek and Egyptian motifs, French Empire designs and Chinese lattice-work, boosted the profits of the cabinetmakers, and the Regent's great building schemes gave the building industry new vigour. Indeed, both his personal extravagance and his public patronage created an immense amount of employment among the working classes for which he was seldom given any credit whatever by his ill-natured critics.

After the battle of Waterloo the building industry prospered as never before. The brick-kilns and lead factories at Islington and all round the edge of the built-up areas worked to capacity and smoked all day and all night, forming 'a ring of fire' round the city. Bricklayers, plasterers, stonemasons and common labourers digging foundations, making roads or moving consignments of heavy material from the docks to the central areas, could earn good wages; and like a stone dropped in a pool, all this intense building activity sponsored by the Regent and his Government, spread in ever widening circles among the peripheral trades of decorating and furnishing, bringing prosperity to the carpet weavers, the upholsterers and curtain makers, the French polishers, the ormolu and brass-workers and Mr James Maclean of 58 Upper Marylebone Street, who claimed 'to finish the smallest articles in the neatest manner'.

Feeding the inhabitants of London also created a vast amount of employment all through the scale from the high-class butchers, fishmongers, grocers and pastrycooks down to the street sellers of oysters, cats' meat and gingerbread. Along the gravel outcrop of the river and at Brompton, Kennington, Lambeth and Earls Court, market gardening predominated. In the clayland of the north, at

Chalk Farm, Belsize Park and Islington the dairy farms were situated, and cows grazed in the lush meadows off Kensington High Street, where, until recently, in a cul-de-sac behind the cinema opposite the gates of Holland Park, a dilapidated cow shed could still be seen. In Fulham, Hammersmith and Chelsea, vegetables were grown in rotation with barley and wheat and the people who hoed the fields followed the pattern of rural life dictated by the seasons. When they drove into the markets in the early morning they brought a breath of country freshness with them, but were a good match for the middle-men bargaining with them over prices.

Bad harvests in 1816 and 1819 sent the price of bread rocketing; dozens of London bakers went bankrupt, while Mr Gunther, the confectioner, grew so rich he was able to build himself a handsome country villa at Earls Court and to enjoy hunting with the aristocracy. Not much was done to alleviate the miseries of the poor. They hung around the taverns and scrabbled among the garbage in the gutters and their big-eyed, pale-faced children went into the 'flash houses' to learn how to pick pockets and steal from the rich without being detected. Perhaps nothing much could be done, for it was not until half a century later when the Victorian conscience became active that the problem of the poor was tackled with firmness. The Victorians built 'model dwellings' for the working classes, Rowton Houses for the homeless and almshouses for the aged, and they also endeavoured to bring the haphazard administration of London under control by removing it from the vestrymen of the individual parishes and creating the Metropolitan Board of Works with responsibility for the sewage, the collection of refuse and the lighting, paving and upkeep of the streets. To some extent they succeeded in bringing the corrupt and turbulent underworld of the Regency within the boundaries of law and order, or when they failed in their purpose, pushed it out of sight into the decaying limbo of back streets and alleys still abounding in their capital city.

CHAPTER NINE

Some Visitors
to London

Very few of the visitors who came to London ever penetrated its darkest corners. Prince Pückler-Muskau was an exception. Curiosity took him once to 'a sort of a barn, very dirty and with holes in the roof which let in the moonlight', to see a fine terrier dog, called Billy, kill a hundred rats in ten minutes. The arena on the floor of the barn was surrounded by a gallery, filled 'with the lowest vulgar and with perilous-looking faces of both sexes', and a ladder led up to a higher gallery 'for the patrician part of the spectators', paying 3s. a seat. 'There was a strange contrast between the fashionables and the populace . . . who were continually offering bets from twenty or fifty pounds', and when a strong man appeared carrying a sack of live rats, the excitement was intense. The moment the rats were let loose, the dog rushed in and slaughtered them one after the other and no sooner had it accounted for the rats than it was set on again to fight a badger in a hideous, bloodthirsty combat, which the Prince called 'a most singular exhibition'. He did not like it—and no wonder. These cruel and horrible amusements, dating from the earliest times, had been declared illegal and were slowly dying out in London, but with cock-fighting and bull-baiting, could still be found in the secret and most dingy quarters of the suburbs.

Pückler-Muskau enjoyed the exhibition of the wild beasts at Exeter 'Change in the Strand a good deal more and was impressed by the huge old lion, called Nero. And there were occasions when this fastidious, Teutonic prince thought he preferred the animal kingdom to English society. He found the ladies in particular, with a few exceptions, both frivolous and cold; but as he had come to London with the set purpose of marrying an heiress to get himself out of his financial troubles and with the intention of taking his new bride home to live *à trois* with the divorced wife he adored in his remote castle at Muskau, it may well be that the ladies disliked his one-sided idea of a good bargain.

As a foreigner and a prince, even of a small and somewhat obscure German principality, his entrée into Society was assured. He was invited everywhere, being on good terms with Countess Lieven, Prince Esterhazy and his lady and the rest of the *corps diplomatique*. 'More than forty invitations are now lying on my table,' he wrote, 'five or six for each day': a soirée at Lady Cowper's, another at Prince Polignac's, and a private concert in Grosvenor Square, where 'the rooms were chokeful and several young men lay on the carpet at the feet of their ladies, with their heads luxuriously reclined against the cushions of the sofas on which their fair ones are seated'. This 'Turkish fashion' he considered to be quite delightful, and he much preferred this kind of entertainment to 'the ludicrous routs, at which one hardly finds standing-room on the staircase and where one pushes and is pushed and kept for hours in a hot-house temperature'. Many

Fig. 53 *A Peep at the Gaslights in Pall Mall. By Rowlandson, 1809*
(Mansell Collection)

K

of the ladies and even some of the gentlemen fainted in the crush at these overcrowded assemblies and it was impossible for them to find their carriages in the street outside so great was the confusion, with the coachmen swearing at each other and trying to force their way up to the door.

The Prince, however, enjoyed London at night and was extremely enthusiastic about the splendid lighting in the streets of the West End (*Fig. 53*). Gas lamps, in spite of fierce opposition from the whale-oil industry and much ridicule from the public and the cartoonists, had been installed in Pall Mall by private enterprise in 1807, and before long the new form of lighting was extended to replace the feeble flicker of the old oil-lamps and their foul smell. The Gas Light & Coke Company received its charter from Parliament in 1812, built the first gas works near the Regent's Canal, and in three years laid twenty-eight miles of gas piping under the streets of London. The parish of St Margaret's Westminster was the first to go over to the new lighting, which was far in advance of anything to be seen in the Continental cities and considered to be one of the wonders of the world. Lamps of all designs in wrought iron, copper and bronze came on the market and elegant lamp-posts were forged out of the French and English cannon scrapped after the battle of Waterloo. Some of these—and the street bollards having a similar origin—can still be seen in Regent's Park and in St James's around Clarence House, marked with the royal cypher of George IV.

All the best houses, the clubs and the shops went over to gas-lighting and according to Pückler-Muskau, the effect was astonishing. 'The convenient walking on the excellent *trottoirs*, the gay and ever-changing groups of people and the numerous splendid shops make the streets of London in the evening a very agreeable walk for a foreigner,' he reported. 'Besides the brilliant gas-lights, there are large globes of glass in the druggists' shops filled with liquid of a deep red, blue or green colour, the splendid light of which is visible for miles and often serves as a beacon.' Then there were the shops dealing in lamps, 'affording a display which it would not be easy to find on the Continent', and the shops where the best English glass was sold, the lustres dazzling like diamonds or coloured like rubies and sapphires and tastefully combined to look like 'clusters of flowers from an oriental garden'.

One evening the Prince rode round Westminster in the moonlight and was fascinated by 'the numerous lights on board the vessels dancing like Will-o'-the-Whisps on the surface of the Thames and the many bridges spanning the noble stream as with arches of light'. On other occasions he explored Regent's Park and Chelsea and went off to Southwark to look at Barclay's Brewery, where he saw 20,000 quarts of beer being boiled and cooled in four huge vats before being run off into barrels, and some of the dray horses, 'as big as elephants', used for delivering the beer. Everything was done by machinery, powered by a single steam engine, and was on such a vast scale, the Prince vowed he had never seen anything like it before. And indeed, his admiration for the inventive skill of the British in developing all kinds of new machines was unbounded. He went to an exhibition in the Strand of the very latest mechanical devices and saw, among other things, 'a very compendious domestic telegraph, which spares the servants half their labour and us nearly all their burdensome presence, a washing machine which requires only one woman to wash a great quantity of linen and a most elegant churn, with which you can make butter on your breakfast table in two minutes'.

He admired also the quality and the service of the hotels he stayed in. The appointments were far more luxurious than anything to be found on the Continent. 'Not one miserable water-bottle, with a single earthen or silver jug and basin, and a long strip of towel such as you are given in all the hotels in France and Germany,' he wrote, 'but positive tubs of handsome porcelain, in which you may plunge half your body; cocks which instantly supply you with streams of water at pleasure; half a dozen wide towels; a multitude of fine glass bottles and glasses, great and small; a large standing looking-glass, foot baths etc., not to mention other anonymous conveniences of the toilet, all of equal elegance.' Moreover, the pretty chambermaids dropped him a curtsey when they came into his room and although he thought English servants expected too many 'vails' (or tips), the waiters in the dining-room treated him with a proper respect.

All these improvements in serving the visitors to London were new. It was only in the Napoleonic Wars that the first fashionable hotels had been set up to provide high-class accommodation for the officers of the army and the navy returning home on leave. They were small, elegant establishments situated in the most expensive area of the town around St James's Street and Piccadilly, more exclusive than the coaching inns, which, however, began to adopt the more snobbish title of Hotel, and more convenient for travellers making a short stay in the metropolis than the business of hiring lodgings. The St James's Royal Hotel (*Fig. 54*) kept by J. C. English, Symon's, Ellis's and Fenton's Hotel were all on the west side of St James's Street, Fenton's

Fig. 54 *St James's Royal Hotel* (Mansell Collection)

having started in the eighteenth century as a fashionable lounge known as Perault's or Pero's Bagnio, where a cold bath could be had for 2s. 6d. and a warm one for 5s.

Captain Gronow, after returning from Paris in 1814, enjoyed 'the capital English dinner' which old James, the waiter at Fenton's, provided to celebrate his victorious progress with the allied armies through Europe. But then—as now—the waiters gave special service to their regular customers. At Stephen's Hotel in Bond Street, another favourite resort of the Guards officers and the dandies, if a stranger asked to dine there, he was stared out of countenance and solemnly informed that no table was vacant. 'It was not an uncommon thing to see 30 or 40 saddle-horses and tilburies waiting outside this hotel,' Gronow reported; and he remembered that two of his Welsh friends while they were staying there, used to dispose of five bottles of wine each every day. 'The familiar joints, boiled fish and fried soles were the only eatables you could order' at Stephen's, but greater variety was to be found on the menu at some of the other hotels, especially at Grenier's in Jermyn Street and at the Clarendon in Bond Street, run by Jacquiers, a refugee from the French Revolution, whose cooking was superb. Here 'you could be sure of getting a genuine French dinner, never costing less than £3 or £4 a head, with a good bottle of claret or champagne at a guinea'.

Dining out and staying in the best hotels was not a very cheap amusement, and the tipping or 'vails' that Prince Pückler-Muskau complained of, could become exceedingly expensive. Byron was in the habit of tipping the staff with a reckless generosity, but even before he was well-known, he expected and got the maximum amount of attention. On his first visit to London in the summer of 1807 at the age of nineteen, he spent a month at Gordon's Hotel in Arlington Street: 'In a perpetual vortex of dissipation,' he wrote, 'very pleasant for all that—routs, balls and boxing-matches, cards, crim. cons., aquatic races, love and lotteries'. And when he returned from his tour in the Near East four years later, he went to Reddish's Hotel in St James's Street, arriving with an incredible amount of baggage, including among other things, a silver funerary urn, four Athenian skulls, some live tortoises, a phial of Attic hemlock and the manuscript of *Childe Harold's Pilgrimage*, which was soon to make him famous. The more permanent lodgings he took at No. 8 St James's Street and then at No. 4 Bennett Street near by, were besieged by crowds hoping to catch a glimpse of him as he strolled out and went limping down Piccadilly to Watier's dining and gambling club, or across to Albemarle Street to call on John Murray.

Murray, by then the most influential publisher in London, used his drawing-room as a meeting place for all the distinguished men of letters who had become his friends, and it was here in 1815 that he introduced Sir Walter Scott to Byron. 'Report had prepared me to meet a man of peculiar habits and quick temper, and I had some doubts whether we were likely to suit each other,' Scott wrote afterwards, 'but I was most agreeably disappointed in this respect. I found Lord Byron in the highest degree courteous and even kind.' Indeed, they took to each other immediately in spite of being totally different in temperament and 'found a great deal to say to each other', meeting almost daily for an hour or two's intimate conversation and very often at the same parties in the evenings; for Scott had already become a celebrity after the success of *The Lay of the Last Minstrel* and *The Lady of the Lake*, and he enjoyed the fuss everyone made of him without ever allowing it to turn his head.

As early as 1809 when he was staying with his friends the Dumergues in Piccadilly, he would joke about 'playing the lion' like Snug, the joiner, in *A Midsummer Night's Dream*. 'If people are amused with hearing me tell a parcel of old stories or recite a pack of ballads to lovely young girls and gaping matrons, they are easily pleased,' he declared, 'and a man would be very ill-natured who would not give pleasure so cheaply conferred.' Later he kept everyone, including the Prince Regent, guessing about the authorship of *Waverley* and his other novels, and this added a romantic aura of mystery to his personality, which excited even more curiosity. 'Make up your mind to be stared at only a little less than the Czar of Muscovy or old Blucher,' his devoted friend Joanna Baillie, who lived in Hampstead, wrote before his visit coinciding with the Allied Sovereigns; and no less a person than the Prince Regent himself was writing at the same time through his librarian and domestic chaplain, the Rev. J. S. Clarke, that he was 'very desirous of seeing him at Carlton House, having long been an enthusiastic admirer of his work'.

When Scott eventually arrived in London, the Prince invited him to what he called 'a snug little dinner' at Carlton House, limiting the company to a small number of guests so that the party would not be overshadowed by court etiquette; and according to Croker, who was there, the Prince and Scott were 'enchanted' with each other. 'Both were brilliant story-tellers in their several ways and both exerted themselves that evening with delightful effect.' The one slightly awkward moment at midnight, when the Prince called for a bumper and charged his glass to 'the author of *Waverley*', was artfully turned by Scott, who kept his secret without offending his royal host. As a testimony of his high opinion of his genius, the Prince gave his favourite author a gold snuff-box with a medallion portrait of himself set in diamonds in the lid; but Scott would not be drawn when friends tried to probe him for his opinion on the Prince's talents beyond stating that 'he conversed with so much ease and elegance it was impossible not to admire him as a well-bred and accomplished English gentleman'.

Scott usually put up at Long's Hotel in Bond Street or stayed with friends in London, travelling down from the North by sea with his wife and their eldest daughter. But after Sophia had married James Lockhart, he always stayed at their house in Sussex Place, Regent's Park. By then his wife had died and the financial collapse of his Edinburgh publisher, Constable, had altered his circumstances considerably, though not his personal integrity or, when he could tear himself away from his beloved Abbotsford, his enjoyment of London society. In spite of all his anxieties and of working harder than ever to pay off his debts, he took great pleasure in dining at Holland House or with Mrs Arbuthnot and the Duke of Wellington and in breakfasting with Samuel Rogers, where he met Luttrell, Sir Thomas Lawrence and Tom Moore. He was extremely fond of Tom Moore and thought he had been badly treated over Byron's *Memoirs*. Under the flippant man-of-the-world manner of the Irish poet with his songs and his frivolous gaiety, his snobbery and his sentimentality, he detected 'a good-humoured fellow' like himself, who could laugh at being lionized and did not 'walk with his nose in the air'.

The author of *Waverley* never met the bright-eyed author of *Sense and Sensibility*, but Scott admired Jane Austen's work enormously. 'The Big Bow-wow strain I can do myself like anyone now going,' he wrote, 'but the exquisite touch, which renders ordinary commonplace things and characters interesting from the truth of the description and the sentiment, is denied me.' The comic irony and wit of the rector of Steventon's daughter were likewise outside his range as a novelist, but Jane shared with Scott the wish to remain anonymous when her first book appeared and it was her brother Henry who negotiated the publication of *Sense and Sensibility* with Mr Thomas Egerton of the Military Library in Whitehall. The proofs began to arrive when she was staying with Henry and his wife at their house in Sloane Street in the spring of 1811, and she was quite naturally very excited, though rather dubious about the future of her book. 'I can no more forget it than a mother can forget her sucking child,' she wrote to her sister Cassandra, and this in spite of the giddy round of amusements organized by Henry and Eliza for her entertainment.

Eliza gave 'a grand Party' in Sloane Street for sixty-six people, who filled the back drawing-room and overflowed into the passage leading to a smaller room at the front. 'The rooms were dressed up with flowers etc. and looked very pretty, and a glass for the Mantle-piece was lent by the man who is making one for Henry.' But Jane could not resist poking fun at the whole affair. 'At ½ past 7 arrived the Musicians in two Hackney coaches,' she wrote, 'and by 8 the lordly company began to appear. . . . I was quite surrounded by acquaintances, especially gentlemen.' The music consisted of 'Lessons on the Harp, or the Harp and Piano Forte together—and the Harp Player was Wiepart, whose name seems famous . . . and there was one female singer, a short Miss Davis all in blue, whose voice was said to be very fine indeed.' The party was reported in the *Morning Post* the next day, which was a feather in Eliza Austen's cap.

Henry was a regular playgoer and a connoisseur of acting. He took his sister to see Dowton and Mathews in an anglicized version of *Tartuffe*, but they missed Mrs Siddons as Queen Constance because of a rumour that she was not well enough to appear that evening. Friends invited Jane to dinner or to drink tea with them and

131

Fig. 55 *Harding, Howell & Co, a linen-drapers in Pall Mall. By Ackermann, 1809* (Hulton Picture Library)

she went to an exhibition of watercolours with Henry, which they both enjoyed. On Sunday she walked in Kensington Gardens, where the lilacs were already in bloom, and during the week she went in and out of the shops (*Fig. 55*). 'I am sorry to tell you that I am getting very extravagant and spending all my money,' she informed Cassandra, 'and what is worse for *you*, I have been spending all yours too; for in a Linendraper's Shop to which I went for check'd muslin and for which I was obliged to give seven shillings a yard, I was tempted by a pretty coloured muslin with a small red spot and bought 10 yds of it, on the chance of your liking it.' Bonnets were extremely tempting, also. Miss Burton, the milliner, made Jane a very pretty one and agreed to make her a straw hat 'of the riding hat shape', for 'nothing can now satisfy me but I must have a straw hat,' she confessed. 'I am really very shocking, but it will not be dear at a guinea.'

Not only the fashions in London, 'the Bugle Trimming at 2s 4d and the Pelisses at 17s, with very expensive buttons', but the splendid showrooms of Mr Wedgwood in York Street, St James's Square, were irresistible to anyone coming from the quiet provincial background of Chawton in Hampshire, and it was not surprising if Jane was in a constant flutter about spending too much money. In fact, she need not have worried, for instead of *Sense and Sensibility* making a loss, which she would have had to repay to Mr Egerton, it made her a profit of £140. *Pride and Prejudice*, published in 1813, was even more successful and so highly praised by a great number of people, that Henry, 'in his Brotherly vanity and love', could not keep the secret any longer. Even so Jane refused steadily to exploit her fame and made no attempt to conquer high society during her visits to London, being content to shine within her own circle of friends and relations.

Recognition, however, came quite unexpectedly from the highest in the land in 1815 when Jane was staying with Henry at 23 Hans Place, the house he had moved into after the death of his wife. *Mansfield Park* had already followed *Pride and Prejudice* and Jane was in the act of going over to John Murray as the publisher of her fourth novel, *Emma*, when Henry fell ill and was treated by an excellent young surgeon called Mr Haden, who, it transpired, was acquainted with one of the Prince Regent's physicians. Mr Haden, it seems, mentioned the fact that his new patient, Henry Austen, had a sister called Jane, which led to the discovery that the Prince was such a great admirer of her work he kept a set of her novels in each of his residences. This overwhelming news, carried to Hans Place by the obliging Mr Haden, was followed almost immediately by a letter from the Rev J. S. Clarke inviting Jane to visit the library at Carlton House and intimating that the dedication of her next book to His Royal Highness would not be found unacceptable.

Jane received 'many flattering attentions' from the Rev J. S. Clarke when she visited Carlton House, but left no record of how its hot-house splendours impressed her lively mind. She, of course, accepted the honour of dedicating *Emma* to the Prince, giving John Murray strict instructions that a presentation copy of the three volumes, bound in morocco and stamped in gold, should be sent to Carlton House three days before publication. She was, however, far too sensible and far too shrewd to be taken in by the Rev J. S. Clarke's suggestion that her next work should be 'an historical romance, illustrative of the history of the august House of Coburg', which might be dedicated to Prince Leopold, then about to marry the Regent's daughter, Princess Charlotte. 'I could not sit seriously down to write a serious romance under any other motive than to save my life,' she told him, 'and if it were indispensible for me to keep it up and never relax into laughing at myself or at other people, I am sure I should be hung before I had finished the first chapter.' She knew exactly where her talent lay and no amount of flattery from the Prince's domestic chaplain could induce her to promise what she knew she could not perform. In fact her life was almost over and her visits to London at an end. She died in 1817 at the age of forty-one, a few months before the Princess Charlotte, whose death in childbirth at the age of twenty-one plunged the nation and her young husband into an agony of grief.

Prince Leopold had paid his first visit to London with the Allied Sovereigns in 1814. He was a handsome, bewhiskered young man in his early twenties, belonging to the small and impoverished German principality of Saxe-Coburg. As a somewhat insignificant member of the Emperor Alexander's suite, he could find no room at the Pulteney Hotel and was not invited to stay at Carlton House, so he lodged for the time being very cheaply above a grocer's shop in the Marylebone High Street. He was rather good at watching the antics of royalty from the sidelines, and towards the hoydenish, erratic daughter of the Regent his behaviour was exemplary. He saw her chasing Prince Augustus of Russia, another of the visiting royalties, and knew something of her obstinate refusal of the marriage which the Regent had concocted for his daughter with the ugly and stupid Prince of Orange. She was plainly unreliable. There had been trouble with her mother and trouble with the Regent himself in his relations with the Princess, but she was popular with the nation and heiress to the most powerful kingdom in the world. Alone, in his room in Marylebone, the Prince of Coburg bided his time and made a few calculations, which he confided to no one except Baron Stockmar, his trusted adviser; and it was, therefore, no surprise to either of them when the next invitation he received to visit London came from the Regent himself in 1816, intimating that it was his wish to give the young man his daughter's hand in marriage.

The marriage was extremely happy. Princess Charlotte settled down with her husband at Claremont, a few miles outside London, and in due course the prospect of her giving birth to an heir was greeted with joy. Everything seemed to be going well. Sir Richard Croft, the obstetrician, went into residence at Claremont in October, but on November 5 the Princess gave birth to a stillborn son and early the next morning she died. Londoners were shocked and horrified. 'No description in the papers can exaggerate the public sympathy and the public sorrow,' Benjamin Haydon declared. 'The nation would have resigned all the rest of her family to have saved her. The loss of the dear Princess Charlotte to us is irreparable.'

And so it was. To the Radicals, the middle classes and all those who thought the Regent's extravagance intolerable, the Princess had been the one hope of the future.

The Regent was blamed for being at the Marquis of Hertford's shoot in Suffolk instead of at Claremont at the crucial moment and his popularity suffered a sharp decline. The scurrilous cartoonists, the pamphleteers and the mob gave him no peace. No wonder he went into hiding and shut himself up with Nash and his maps and his elevations; no wonder he kept his ministers waiting while he talked to his tailor about the design of a new dress coat for the Hussars. Life at the top was not easy for this emotional extrovert with the mind and talents of an artist and the responsibilities of a constitutional monarch. Even his relaxations were criticized, his love of music no less than his passion for architecture; when he entertained Rossini, it was said that he allowed the Italian composer too much familiarity because he enjoyed singing duets with him.

Rossini came to London in December 1823, with his former mistress Madame Colbran, who was now his wife. They had such a terrible Channel crossing, the composer arrived in a state of nervous collapse and for more than a fortnight could not be persuaded to leave his lodgings at No. 90 Regent Street, where he took to his bed, or was sometimes to be seen sitting on the balcony above Nash's colonnade with a pet parrot at his side, apparently intent on watching the traffic below. When he finally emerged, his fascinating personality won him great popularity and he was much sought after by fashionable society. No smart musical party was complete without him and as he insisted on a minimum fee of £50 for the joint appearance of himself and his wife, they made a great deal of money. Madame Colbran was rather *passée*, but this made no difference at all. The public concert given at Almack's for their mutual benefit was packed to the doors and Rossini, as well as accompanying his wife, sang several of the familiar arias from his celebrated operas.

Foreign musicians tended to look on London as a milch-cow. Nowhere else in the world could they obtain such high fees both in public and in private; for the appetite for music in the metropolis was insatiable and the snobbery of the élite encouraged them to favour the performers and composers with a Continental reputation rather than the struggling musicians of their native country, whose status was little better than a servant's. Felix Mendelssohn on his first visit in 1829, met with as much approval as Rossini. The son of a banker, he was young, highly educated, handsome and elegant.

135

Moreover, he could dance and ride a horse and even speak English tolerably well, which meant that the aristocracy found him congenial and could look upon him almost—if not quite—as one of themselves.

He had friends in London: Ignaz Moscheles, the German pianist, and Karl Klingemann, a diplomat, who found him lodgings at 103 Great Portland Street and took him under their wing. They arranged for him to visit the Italian opera at the King's Theatre in the Haymarket to hear the incomparable Malibran in Rossini's *Otello*, took him to see Charles Kemble as Hamlet at Covent Garden, and got him invited to a ball at the Duke of Devonshire's. London fascinated and bewildered him. 'It is fearful! It is mad! I am quite giddy and confused,' he wrote home to his family. 'London is the grandest and the most complicated monster on the face of the earth. . . . Things toss and whirl about me as if I were in a vortex, and I am whirled along with them. In the last six months in Berlin I have not seen so many contrasts and so much variety as in these three days. Just turn to the right from my lodging, walk down Regent Street and see the wide, bright thoroughfare with its arcades (alas! it is again enveloped in thick fog today) and the shops with signs as big as a man, and the stage-coaches piled high with people. . . . See how a horse rears up in front of a house because his rider has friends there; and how men are used for carrying advertisements extolling the achievements of performing cats; and the beggars and those fat John Bulls with their slender, beautiful daughters hanging on their arms. Ah, those daughters!'

Mendelssohn was susceptible to feminine beauty and a romantic, but the president of the Philharmonic Society, Sir George Smart, was quite mistaken in thinking he was a rich playboy fooling about in society and not a serious musician. He had to reverse his opinion altogether when Mendelssohn gave his first concert with the Philharmonic Society at the Hanover Rooms, London's premier concert hall in Hanover Square. The fashionable audience went mad about the young composer, whose C Minor Symphony had never before been heard in London, and Mendelssohn himself gave high praise to the orchestra for their excellent performance. A few weeks later he appeared as a solo pianist at the Argyle Rooms in Regent Street and followed this with another very successful concert with the Philharmonic Society when he conducted his new Overture to *A Midsummer Night's Dream*. Unfortunately in all the excitement after the concert, his English friend, Thomas Attwood, left the one and only copy of this score on the seat of a hackney carriage, which trotted off and was never seen again, so that Mendelssohn had to sit down and rewrite the Overture from memory.

With the London Season at an end, he went off on a tour of Scotland and Wales, but when he returned to the capital in September he was thrown out of a carriage and laid up for weeks with a bad leg. His first drive out of doors when he was getting better, moved him deeply. 'The sun shone on me and the sky did me the favour of being a deep blue,' he wrote. 'London was indescribably beautiful. The red and brown chimney-pots contrasted so sharply with the blue sky, and all the colours glowed, the gay shops gleamed and the blue air poured out of every cross street and enveloped the background. Instead of the green, fluttering leaves I last saw from my gig I now saw red sticks standing up stiffly, and only the lawns were still green. How beautifully the roses in Piccadilly gleamed in the sunshine, and how full of variety everything seemed! It gave me a strange but very comforting sensation and I felt the power of returning health. I shall bring away very dear memories of this town, and when I drive off on the stage-coach (or rather inside, for I am a "burnt child") I shall look back many a time and think of the pleasure I have had here. For indeed it does one's heart good when people are friendly and loyal, and it gives me the deepest pleasure to be able to say honestly that they are so here.'

Mendelssohn never revised this verdict. He loved London and always felt at home there.

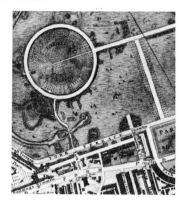

CHAPTER TEN

An Expanding City

By 1830 when George IV died, the major Regency improvements in the centre of London were almost complete and the built-up area had been greatly extended. Horwood's *Plan of the Cities of London and Westminster* of 1794 had been superseded by the publication in 1827 of Greenwood's *Map of London*, based on a new survey and showing the very considerable growth that had taken place in the years between.

Open fields and farmlands on Horwood's map had been filled in by the time Greenwood made his survey with the final development of the Bloomsbury Estate as far as Euston Square and St Pancras village and with the less crowded developments of Regent's Park and St John's Wood. South of Hyde Park the fields belonging to Earl Grosvenor were likewise disappearing in the new residential district of Belgravia, reaching down to Pimlico and the village of Chelsea and linking up with the eastern edge of Henry Holland's Hans Town. South of the river the radial roads from the new bridges built in the Waterloo period were fringed by terraces of houses with large gaps in between, like an irregular string of beads stretching through Lambeth and Kennington and the Elephant and Castle as far as the villages of Camberwell, Peckham and Dulwich. In the East End on both sides of the river, sporadic developments influenced by the commercial complex of the new docks made a network of new and old streets sprawling untidily through Stepney and Bow, or clustered round the naval dockyard at Deptford and the splendid buildings at Greenwich.

There were still fields and farms round Paddington, Westbourne Green, Kilburn, Kentish Town and other areas on the rural fringe. But the population had increased from about 800,000 in 1800 to more than 1,400,000 in the thirty odd years between Horwood and Greenwood and the corresponding development of London had moved at a startling pace. Some architects and planners thought it had gone far enough and one of them actually suggested that an attempt should be made to contain the city by establishing an artificial limit at the western boundary of Hyde Park. This, however, made no impression, for the speculation in land and housing yielded far too much profit to the great landowners and the builders themselves for any limit to be recognized or enforced, and many of the most characteristic features of London belong to this period when the influence of the Regency style was still paramount.

Thomas Cubitt, following the example of James Burton, organized himself and his younger brother Lewis into a formidable building company with large workshops in the Gray's Inn Road, employing a permanent staff of bricklayers, masons and allied tradesmen on a bigger scale than had ever been known before. To keep his organization moving he was constantly on the lookout for any available land that he could lease for building; and having already developed parts of Highbury and Stoke Newington very successfully, he took over what was left of the Bedford Estate in Bloomsbury when James Burton became absorbed in his other commitments in Regent's Park. Unhappily, owing to the depredations of London University, bulldozing its way like an angry elephant through the pleasant squares and terraces of Bloomsbury, only a few bits and pieces of Cubitt's work can now be seen in Tavistock Square, Endsleigh Street, Gordon Square and the charming little shopping precinct of Woburn Walk lying behind the great church of St Pancras built in 1820.

Bloomsbury, however, was only one of Cubitt's speculations. The conversion of Buckingham House into Buckingham Palace from 1821 onwards, gave a new importance to the district lying to the west of it, comprising the 'five fields' belonging to Lord Grosvenor and the low-lying pastures of Pimlico. Cubitt immediately saw the possibilities of the site and took nineteen acres on a long lease. Two Swiss financiers, George and William Haldimand, joined him in a syndicate to undertake the first major development of the area in Belgrave Square (*Fig. 56*), which was designed by Soane's most brilliant pupil, George Basevi. With its superb Graeco-Roman blocks of houses in gleaming stucco and its three large individual mansions, the Square has survived, its grandeur undiminished by the number of motor-cars parked round its central garden; and while Basevi went on to design the elegant Pelham Crescent in South Kensington, Cubitt continued to

Fig. 56 *Belgrave Square* (Photo: A. F. Kersting)

work on his plans for the rest of Belgravia and Pimlico, building Eaton Square and the surrounding streets in a style worthy of Nash at his best and with a solidity that this great *entrepreneur* of the Regency so often lacked.

Belgravia was the grandest and the most successful of the metropolitan estates built in the late 1820s and the 1830s. Many others were contemplated and begun at the same time on a more modest scale to satisfy the housing needs of the middle classes, notably the Bishop of London's Paddington Estate round Sussex Square, of which very little remains, and the smaller estates off Kensington Gore, Kensington High Street, the Brompton Road (*Fig. 57*), Holland Park and Campden Hill, where many attractive Regency squares and houses can still be found.

Meanwhile, in the area north-west of Regent's Park, known as St John's Wood, a new type of development had begun on the Eyre Estate and the land belonging to the Keepers and Governors of Harrow School. It is not known who conceived the original idea of building pairs of semi-detached villas standing in their own grounds instead of the more usual terraces or blocks of houses going up all over London; but this was the innovation adopted from the first plan sketched out for the Eyre Estate in 1794 when it finally came to be developed in the 1820s and 1830s. Some of the semi-detached villas were built in the neo-Classical style of the Regency with graceful wrought-iron balconies, bow-windows and elegant porticoes; others with the pointed gables, Gothic windows and castellated roof lines

140

of the *cottage ornée*, reminiscent of the style popularized by Nash in his early days in Wales and Herefordshire and pointing the way towards the Gothic revival, besides inaugurating a pattern of suburban development which has been followed ever since with some good and some very bad results.

St John's Wood, in spite of the erection of large featureless blocks of flats on the main roads running through it, still retains much of its unique character and some of the most delightful private gardens in London. In the 1830s the Eyre Arms Tavern and Tea Gardens marked the northern boundary of the Estate, and the ponds attached to the farm behind what is now the Tube station, still served as a watering-place for cattle. The wide tree-lined avenue of Hamilton Terrace on the Harrow School Estate was begun before Greenwood's map of 1827 with the two small terraces of brick houses and pairs of larger houses at the southern end, the rest of the street being marked with a dotted line between the orchards and the fields stretching down to Pineapple Place and Maida Vale; and at the same time the original track from the Edgware Road passing the boundary of Lord's Cricket Ground and running eastwards through another farm called Punker's Barn to the new burial ground outside Regent's Park, was widened into the St John's Wood Road. The young painter, Edwin Landseer, bought the rustic cottage and outbuildings of Punker's Barn in 1824 for £100 for conversion into a studio and lived there until his death fifty years later, by which time the pleasant area behind his house

Fig. 57 *Brompton in 1822. By George Scharf* (Hulton Picture Library)

L

reaching down to the Regent's Canal and known as North Bank, was in the process of being totally destroyed by the building of the Great Central Railway.

The St John's Wood Road can still boast of a few Regency houses thought to have been designed by Decimus Burton, and the chapel, now the St John's Wood parish church, still stands among the tombstones of the burial ground. It was built by Thomas Hardwick in 1814, shortly before he started work on the new parish church of St Marylebone facing the entrance to Regent's Park at York Gate, and before the Church Building Act of 1818 had become law. This Act set aside the sum of £1,000,000 for the purpose of providing new churches all over London to serve the needs of the expanding population and was a shrewd political move to offset the spread of Nonconformity by glamorizing the image of the Established Church. More than £50,000 was spent on St Marylebone, while over £70,000 was required to finish the large new church at St Pancras designed by William Inwood and his son.

Young Inwood had travelled in Greece and studied the Periclean temples of Athens. He borrowed his caryatid tribunes from the Erechtheum and his tower was modelled on the Tower of the Winds in Athens (*Fig. 58*), but it rides successfully above the majestic portico. This leads into an octagonal vestibule, preceding the main body of the church, which opens out in a great airy space terminating in a semi-circular apse with six verd-antique scagliola columns. The interior has been most beautifully restored; the exterior is hemmed in by inferior buildings. Even so, St Pancras remains a splendidly original achievement, surpassing all the other churches built under the Act of 1818 by the intensity of feeling expressed through its high architectural quality.

Not much feeling was shown by the other architects who accepted commissions under the Church Building Act, though more than thirty large churches costing between £15,000 and £20,000 were built in various parts of London to accommodate congregations of some eighteen hundred or two thousand worshippers. Soane tried his hand at St Peter's, Walworth, and more successfully at Holy Trinity, Marylebone, now dwarfed by the commercial skyscrapers of the Euston Road. Smirke designed St Anne's, Wandsworth and St Mary's, Wyndham Place, with a handsome semi-circular portico and a rather less attractive tower, which, none the less, enhances the vista from Bryanston Square. Four large churches in South London in the parish of Lambeth, were built at the same time and known as

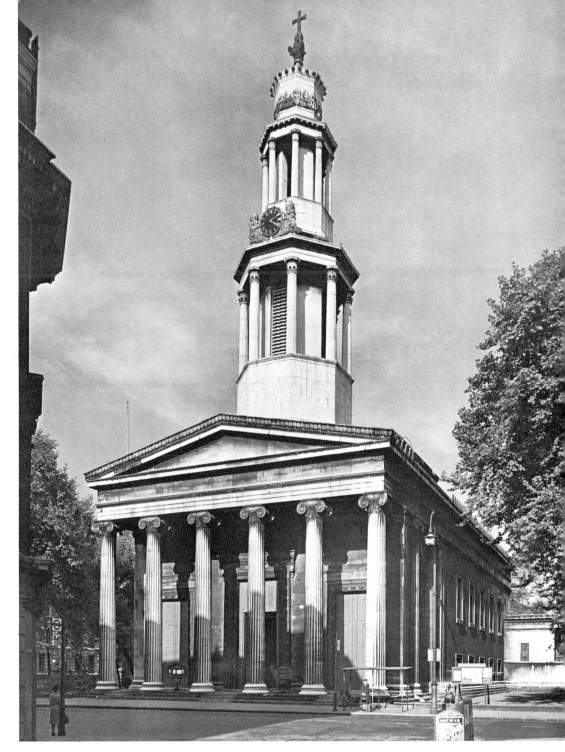

Fig. 58 *St Pancras Church* (Photo: A. F. Kersting)

Fig. 59 *A Regency house on Downshire Hill, Hampstead* (Photo: Michael Taylor) (London Weekend Television)

the Waterloo churches: St Matthew's, Brixton, St Mark's, Kennington, St Luke's, West Norwood and St John's, Waterloo Road. But none of these can be said to match the glory of Wren, Hawksmoor and Gibbs in the previous centuries, perhaps because religion had become a more complacent affair by 1818.

The more simple, less 'official' churches of the Regency, such as Hardwick's chapel in St John's Wood and the small chapel on Downshire Hill in Hampstead, sprang up all over London at this time. St John's, at the angle of Downshire Hill and Keats Grove, was built in 1818 as a chapel of ease for the parish of Hampstead, which by then stretched down to the Lower Heath and Pond Street; for Keats's friends Charles Wentworth Dilke and Charles Armitage Brown were not the only people to share the poet's dislike of being pent up in the city and to prefer living in this delectable area on the edge of the Heath. Most of the charming little houses still to be seen in Keats Grove and Downshire Hill (*Fig. 59*) were built in the Regency, and were occupied by successful tradesmen and their families, doctors, lawyers and other professional people belonging to the middle rank of society.

Like everywhere else, Hampstead was growing rapidly. Higher up, close to the parish church, the Abbé Morel, a refugee from the French Revolution, built a small Roman Catholic church in Holly Place in 1816. Down at North End, in the Vale of Health and on the way up to Hampstead village by Haverstock Hill, small individual houses were dotted about or grouped in clusters by the roadside. Camden Town linked the village to London, but at Chalk Farm cows still grazed in the meadows; and there were fields between Haverstock Hill and Kentish Town, where 'the air was exceedingly wholesome', and the old cottages and new houses were cosy and unpretentious. More pastureland still surrounded Islington farther to the east, though the City, thrusting outwards from Clerkenwell and

Fig. 60 *Highgate Archway designed by Nash in 1813. By James Pollard* (Author's Collection)

Finsbury, had by now reached the Angel, and the residential development of the Canonbury Estate in well-proportioned squares and terraces had begun as early as 1800. The Great North Road from the Angel at Islington was successfully diverted to avoid the long climb up Highgate Hill through a cutting under Hornsey Lane, which was supported by an arch designed by Nash in 1813 (*Fig. 60*).

New roads in the west and the south brought the villages there closer to London and the improvements in transport, with the pair-horse stage coaches covering local journeys, increased their attractions for the well-to-do middle classes. At Fulham there were 'many good buildings belonging to the gentry and the citizens of London'; at Peckham 'many handsome country villas'; at Tooting 'a number of merchant's seats'; at Streatham, where Jane Austen stayed with the Rector and his wife in 1811, a few houses on the edge to the wide common; and at Dulwich, in addition to the old College buildings, the new Art Gallery and Mausoleum designed by Soane in 1812. This was—and still is after restoration of the bomb damage—one of Soane's most brilliant achievements, designed and carried out with the utmost skill and self-assurance, and since the Bank of England has been so much altered, the most eloquent monument to his genius as an architect.

So London developed and grew outwards from the heart of the mercantile City towards the cluster of villages in the still rural country of Middlesex, Essex and Surrey. And with the splendid 'Metropolitan Improvements' of Nash and the Regent, it was more beautiful than it had ever been before—or would ever be again—when the young Queen Victoria moved into Buckingham Palace in 1837.

For Victorian expansion and commercial enterprise were soon to change the whole aspect of London, to maul its Regency elegance and to create a giant metropolis with railways, gas-works, sewage plants, industrial dwellings and pompous or mean middle-class suburbs sprawling out in all directions like the tentacles of an octopus. In spite of the high architectural quality to be found in the Houses of Parliament, the Foreign Office, Tower Bridge, St Pancras Station and the other distinctive landmarks of the Victorian era, an appalling decline in taste set in as the wealth and power of the nation passed from the cultured aristocracy to the *nouveau riche* industrialists. The sure eye of the Regent and his architects and of the speculative builders like James Burton and Thomas Cubitt was clouded over by a pretentious mixture of styles and the mass production of new building materials designed to satisfy the needs of the expanding population at a low cost and with a minimum of aesthetic propriety.

Inundated with a tide of bricks and mortar, London became a shapeless conglomeration as the nineteenth century went on. But the mania for technological 'progress' in the twentieth century has wrought even more harm. The flashy Edwardians had little use for Georgian or Regency architecture, and between the wars it was much abused by the 'modern' architects of the 1920s and 1930s. Regent Street was demolished, Devonshire House destroyed and the elegant houses facing Park Lane, with the exception of those on the corner of Green Street and Upper Brook Street, torn down to make way for flats, hotels and shops. All this and the Blitz in the 1940s should have been enough to satisfy the lust of the vandals. Yet the last thirty years have been even worse; for by submitting to the greed of the developers with their soul-destroying, up-ended monstrosities of concrete and glass, the skyline of London has been raped and the harmonious scale of the squares, the streets and the parks irreparably damaged.

No one would be foolish enough to maintain that a city can go on living without adapting itself to change; but the ruthless, vulgar distortion of London's character in the last three decades has gone far beyond the ordinary process of change. And only now, when it is almost too late, has public opinion in the Preservation Societies, the Borough Councils and the G.L.C. begun to apprehend what is at stake, to realize, moreover, that much of the credit for what remains of the splendour and the beauty of London belongs to the Regent and his architects. They created what our neurotic modern society has singularly failed to achieve—a civilized urban environment.

Index

Pages 154–5. Greenwood's *Map of London*, published 1827, showing the same area as Horwood (pp. ii–iii), with the development of Regent's Park and the area north and north-west of the New Road. (*Guildhall Library*)